The Rise of the
Authoritarian State
in Peripheral Societies

The Rise of the Authoritarian State in Peripheral Societies

Clive Y. Thomas

Monthly Review Press
New York

Library of Congress Cataloging in Publication Data
Thomas, Clive Yolande.
   The rise of the authoritarian state in peripheral societies.

   Bibliography: p.
   Includes index.
   1. Developing countries—Politics and government
2. Authoritarianism—Developing countries. I. Title.
JF60.T46   1984   320.9172'4   84-16490
ISBN 0-85345-657-7
ISBN 0-85345-658-5 (pbk.)

Monthly Review Press
155 West 23rd Street
New York, N.Y. 10011

Manufactured in the United States of America

10 9 8 7 6 5 4 3

To Walter Rodney: revolutionary and scholar

Contents

**Part 2: National Independence
and the Rise of the Authoritarian State**

Preface and Acknowledgments

Despite the obvious importance of those issues that center on the relationship of political democracy—or representative democracy, or, as it is sometimes called, parliamentary democracy—to the projects of socialist transformation and capitalist modernization in the periphery, they have not been adequately discussed in the literature, or, for that matter, sufficiently engaged in the practice of the political organizations in these countries. This is regretable, given the pervasive role that repression plays in the daily lives of their inhabitants and given the great influence exercised by ideological and political debate and struggle over the alternative paths to transformation.

One reason for this state of affairs is the uncritical and naive third worldism that is embraced by many writers on the left. Far too many have been willing to act as cheerleaders for "progressive" regimes, rather than examine the process of transformation in a critical but constructive way. Another reason—and the one that is perhaps the most widespread—is a misunderstanding of the role of political democracy in the advanced capitalist formations.

Propaganda to the contrary notwithstanding, political democracy does not automatically accompany capitalism. Although sometimes referred to as "bourgeois democracy," political democracy, where it is exists, is not the result of bourgeois munificence, but only occurs, and remains, where the workers and popular forces are sufficiently strong to keep it in place. At the successful completion of the industrial revolution, the bourgeoisie never intended to yield ground to the "masses." The long and bitter struggles for the right to vote, to have a "competitive" political system, to independent courts, to trade unions, and so on are a matter of historical record. It was not until well into the present century that the working classes in these countries were able to force a general acceptance of this state form. And despite this success, the record also shows periodic reversals, the most notorious being the fascist interludes in Europe after World War I. The price, therefore, of political democracy is the need for a mass movement, combined with constant vigilance.

In the periphery, there are two attitudes toward political democracy. One is to dismiss it as a purely "bourgeois" deception and to repeat the most naive formulations about democracy being "class determined." This, allied with vulgar interpretations of what a "dictatorship of the proletariat" represents, has paved the way for a very dangerous brand of left authoritarianism.

On the other side we find the "modernists," the ideologues of capitalist development in the periphery who assert that it is only with more (capitalist) development that more democracy can be attained. The problem is thus reduced to mechanical one of simply expanding capitalist penetration. Yet the savage and brutal dictatorships that have developed in Latin America and elsewhere in the third world show only too clearly the falsity of the idea that political democracy is a necessary by-product of capitalist expansion.

This book examines the issues that follow from this general perspective. It seeks to develop a thesis about one particular form of the state—the authoritarian state—which at a particular stage of degeneration of the state in certain of the newly independent societies of Africa, Asia, and the Caribbean. After an introductory chapter that deals with the question of method, there are two parts. In Part 1, the colonial state system is examined in order to unravel the roots of the postcolonial state. It is broken into periods in order to trace these developments in the light of the changing nature of the colonial formation. In Part 2, the central thesis of the authoritarian state is elaborated, along with those issues (including ideology and class structure) that are needed to understand the nature of this form of state power. The final chapter links theory with practice.

While it is impossible to list all those who contributed to the formation of the ideas in this book, two broad sources stand out. First, there is that large community of persons actively engaged in the struggle for a better world whom I have met over the years and conversed or argued with, shared experiences and sometimes struggled with, and who individually and collectively, directly and indirectly, have helped to shape the theory incorporated in this study. To all these, I am deeply indebted—even though the views expressed here do not necessarily represent the positions of any of these people or the organizations they are associated with.

It would seem improbable that, given these many sources of inspiration, any one person could be singled out for individual mention. But Andaiye (who edited the first draft) and Susan Lowes (who edited the final copy) have contributed immeasurably to the clarification of my ideas and to the readability of the text. To both I would like to record my deepest appreciation for the skill and intelligence they contributed to this study; without them, the work would not have appeared. As is always the case, however, I remain finally responsible for the points of view and the manner in which they are expressed.

Introduction

Of the many outstanding features of the Third World, one which is of particular concern is the prevalence of repression, political assassination, disappearances, and the other evidence of installed dictatorships. This feature is prominent both in those countries that have been politically independent for a century and a half—such as Latin America—as well as those that have won their political independence in the post-World War II period. The prevalence of these repressive political forms is the direct counterpart of the absence of internal democratic practices and the virtual outlawing, within these countries, of representative political institutions, multiparty political systems, due process and equality before the law, free and fair elections, and so on. Where repression prevails, the possibility of political and social advances for the broad masses, which seemed imminent as the European empire suffered defeat after defeat after World War II, has also lessened. The Shah in Iran, Papa Doc in Haiti, Idi Amin in Uganda, Pinochet in Chile, Marcos in the Philippines, the Somozas in Nicaragua, and Gairy in Grenada are only a few of the symbols of political terror and brutality that characterize the daily lives of people living in the periphery.

One of the resulting ironies is that within the center countries, despite the fact that their bourgeoisies had, well into the present century, bitterly resisted the social and political advances of their own working classes, and had also pillaged, seized, and colonized the periphery, practiced genocide against their populations, and enslaved them, democratic political norms are today taken as guides to political practice, whereas in the periphery, dictatorial, despotic, and other antipopular measures are the norm of political behavior. In the periphery this holds true both where the regimes describe themselves as capitalist and where they claim to be socialist. For the latter, the identification of the ideals of socialism, peace, equality, and freedom with dictatorial practices seems to raise no particular difficulty, for the "dictatorship of the proletariat" becomes the cover for one-party—and even one-man—rule, while political democracy is dismissed as a "bourgeois illusion" that the masses in a "socialist" country do not need!

If the phenomena referred to here were not so widespread, it might be easier to understand how these regimes are allowed to get away with such nonsense. Unfortunately, however, they are so common that even sympathy with this group of countries— either because of what colonialism heaped on them in the past or because of what imperialism imposes on them today— cannot avoid the somber social reality.

Despite these excesses, little attempt has been made to come to grips with them at a theoretical level. Repression is either explained as being the result of the "backwardness" that is part of being underdeveloped, or as the result of being at a particular stage in development—an evolutionary argument that states that while underdeveloped countries go through a necessary period of rapid modernization, during which the standard of living will be raised, little effort can be spared for the "luxuries" of democracy.

The principal purpose of this book, therefore, is to provide a theoretical analysis of a number of issues relating to the state and politics in peripheral capitalist societies. For reasons that will be made clear later, the book focuses on one category of peripheral capitalist society, the *recent postcolonial society,* and develops a thesis about one set of political-state form that is found among this group of countries, what I call the *authoritarian state.* Since it is my belief that many of the issues raised here are of far-reaching significance for both the theory and practice of politics in these societies, I will begin with a general statement of the reasons why I began the study in the first place and the theoretical and intellectual premises on which it is based.

It should be clear from the preceding that two general sets of factors prompted me to write this book. One is the virtually total absence of democratic political forms in the periphery, which in turn prompts a number of critical theoretical and practical questions about the future direction of political struggle. Principal among these are:

(1) How do we arrive at a correct (and scientific) understanding of the state and politics in the periphery?

(2) What is the relationship between "economic" structure and political and state forms in these societies?

(3) Given such an understanding: (a) Why have repression and state violence been increasing so rapidly? (b) What is the correct relationship between the struggles for the emancipation of the working class and peasantry and the struggles for so-called bourgeois-democratic forms? (c) Can Marxism be indifferent to the forms of the state or the state of legality in the periphery?

(4) Arising out of the above: (a) Are there determinate stages in the struggle to move from variations of peripheral capitalism to the "transition to socialism"? (b) If there are such stages, must they not inform political practice? (c) How contingent are the struggles for emancipation of the working class and peasantry on developments in the so-called center countries and the socialist bloc? (d) What are the consequences for developments in the periphery of the present structural crises of world capitalism?

Questions of a similar nature have been raised in relation to the developed capitalist societies, including the debates that have been raging in Europe on fascism and dictatorship, Eurocommunism, the "British road to socialism," and so on. Given the nature of the center countries, however, the answer to these questions will have little direct applicability to the social context of the societies examined in this essay. In peripheral capitalist societies generally, and even more so in the recent postcolonial ones that are my major concern, such questions have yet to be raised, much less addressed, in a thorough manner. There has been, on the left, what may be termed an instant Utopian vision, which assumes that the capture of state power by a Marxist-led and/or -oriented political party is the immediate task, and that its achievement will be enough to ensure a definitive (although in some cases painful) transition to socialism.

Such naive formulations have been encouraged by the under-development of the Marxist theory of the state and politics, and it is this theoretical underdevelopment that constitutes the second set of factors that prompted this book.

Marxist scholars agree that the Marxist theory of the state and politics is the least developed of the major areas of Marxist scholarship. One reason is that while Marx envisaged an analysis of the bourgeois state as part of his program of work, it was not completed. Most of Marx's political writings were based on concrete events and remain largely fragmentary. In addition, later work by Lenin in this area was also about immediate events, and was of a strongly polemical nature. Various scholars have analyzed this failure. Nicos Poulantzas attributes it to the fact that after Lenin the Internationals tended toward economism, i.e., tended to treat "levels of social reality, including the state [as] simply epiphenomena reducible to the economic 'base.' Thereby a specific study of the state becomes superfluous."[1] Bobbio goes further and believes the underdevelopment is not only of the theory of the bourgeois state and bourgeois democracy but also of the socialist state and socialist democracy.[2] He attributes this to two fatal tendencies. One is that "theorists of socialism have been so concerned with the problem of gaining power, they have tended to emphasize the role of the party rather than the state."[3] The second is that these theorists have assumed that once power is attained, the state will eventually "disappear." H. Goulbourne, writing specifically about peripheral societies, notes that

> politics and the state in Third World countries far too frequently are treated just as aspects of other, albeit interesting, developments. One result of this is the blurring of the importance of the state and politics in these formations in the collections that exist. Of course, this situation reflects, to a large degree, the fact that there is relatively little theorisation of politics and the state in these societies.[4]

There has been more work in this area in recent years, however. In relation to the bourgeois state, the Poulantzas-Miliband debates and the works of the West German "state derivationist" school have covered a significant distance in a short period of time—at least enough so that we should not overstate the lack of theoretical work.[5] In addition, Hal Draper's monumental project, although not yet completed, shows that there is still something of a classical tradition to draw upon, and this is indeed heartening.[6]

If the Marxist theory of state and politics in bourgeois society remains underdeveloped, this is even more pronounced in the literature on the socioeconomic formations of the periphery. Once again, however, this does not mean that there have been no useful contributions. In fact, two broad lines of work can be distinguished. One is associated with the East European thesis of the "noncapitalist path" and represents the official position of the Communist International. It will be examined briefly below. The other includes a rather diverse group of writers and has three broad subtendencies. The first, associated with such names as John Saul, Hamza Alavi, Colin Leys, and Issa Shivji, deals with the recently (post-World War II) independent post-colonial societies of Asia and Africa.[7] The second emerges out of the attempt to apply the work of the state-derivationist school to dependent societies, particularly to those of Latin America.[8] The third derives from the work of those engaged in the "dependency" debate in Latin America and in the application of these ideas to the analysis of the state; the major focus has been on the rise of military dictatorships in Latin America. Much of this literature is vital but not sufficiently accessible to those who do not read Spanish.[9] A great deal of it overlaps with that of the state-derivationist school.

While all these works will be discussed in their appropriate context later in this book, I want to make two general observations here. One is that the work on postcolonial societies has been hampered by the difficulty of making a clear Marxist analysis of the modes of production and social formations in this category. There is a strong tendency to divide the Third World into geographical regions—Africa, Latin America, and so on. While such divisions reflect important differences, equally important differences are found *within* these broad groupings, suggesting a failure to come to grips with the social structure of the periphery. The other observation is more general and is that there has been a tendency to a certain scholasticism in the debates of Marxist political science. The dominant emphasis, particularly in the work on the bourgeois state, has been on surveying political doctrines and making textual exegeses, to the relative neglect of the study of contemporary political forms. As Bobbio has commented, we have

> first-rate books on what Marx or Lenin or Gramsci thought about the state or on a theme of such little contemporaneity as the withering away of the state, but we have neither excellent nor terrible ones dealing with the political systems of states defining themselves as socialist, or with the alternative state of the future—assuming one is not satisfied with those existing today.[10]

On theory

It is a central tenet of this book that a correct theory of politics and the state in peripheral capitalist societies cannot be simply "deduced" from a theory of politics and state in bourgeois society because it must root itself in the concrete conditions of the periphery. Moreover, because of the varied and ubiquitous nature of political relations in these societies, and because of the impact of colonialism on these, there can be no abstract study of the state and politics. The specific nature of each and every state form and the concrete conditions of its politics bear directly on the conclusions of any general theoretical inquiry. One of the continuing weaknesses of the theoretical work on politics in the periphery has been the overemphasis on generalizations and the underemphasis on the real and variegated historical development of these societies. Having said this, however, it should also be noted that there must be a balance between theory and the concrete.

The emphasis in this study is on recent postcolonial societies. But the concepts colonial and postcolonial are not used as mere formal political categories—representing, say, "colonial office rule," or "political independence," or membership/nonmembership in the United Nations and similar bodies. Here colonization refers to the inherent and distinctive historical features of the mediating structures through which the social formations in the periphery have been shaped.

All of the countries of Latin America, the Caribbean, Africa, the Middle East, and Asia have been subject to one form of European colonial domination or another, for periods ranging from a few decades (Syria, Lebanon, etc.), to centuries (Jamaica, Mozambique, etc.). The forms of colonial domination have been varied, ranging from protectorates, mandates, and "unequal treaties" to colonies proper. While political incorporation into the empire of one or another European power has been *sufficient* to ensure the articulation between the precapitalist modes of production found in these societies and the capitalist modes that eventually became dominant in Europe, it has not been a *necessary* condition. The experiences of India and many parts of Africa show that such an articulation often existed prior to formal incorporation into the European empire system. "Recent postcolonial," then, refers specifically to those countries (mainly in Africa, Asia, and the Caribbean) that became independent in the last wave of national liberation struggles that culminated in the final disintegration of the European empires in the post-World War II period. By singling out these societies, we can stress the historically specific influences of colonialism on the development of state forms. The major beneficiaries of the earliest wave of national independence struggles in the late eighteenth and early nineteenth centuries were the countries of Latin America, and there, although the influence of colonialism on the state forms still exists, this influence has been mediated differently, in part because of the longer span of "independence."

It is important to note at this point that by taking this approach I am not setting out to make a historical study of the state and politics of any particular region. I often use the Caribbean as an example, however, both because it is a region I am particularly familiar with and because it offers a unique opportunity to study the impact of colonialism on the development of states in the capitalist periphery, the character of local struggles against colonial domination, and the paths that the decolonization process has followed. This is because the region was colonized early—along with Ireland and the North American colonies, it was part of the first wave of empire building by the world's greatest empire builder, Britain. (The second wave occurred in the last quarter of the eighteenth century and led to the extension of settlement in North America to Canada and the western United States, and the incorporation of India, Australia, the Far East, the South Atlantic, and the west of Africa. The final wave took place in the nineteenth and early twentieth centuries and brought all of the non-European world under one form or another of colonial domination.) In addition to suffering a lengthy period of colonization, the indigenous peoples in the Caribbean were virtually extinguished and European-controlled societies based on immigrant labor created.

Despite its more modest aims, this approach is similar to the use of the historical condition of Britain as the prototype around which Marx developed his analysis in *Capital*. Methodologically, this approach allows the work to be concrete and abstract at the same time: concrete in that the categories used will be derived from real historical experience and abstract in the sense that they will be presented as historical materialist categories derived from the study of social development in its general (and hence abstract) form. Such an approach makes it possible to demonstrate that despite the notoriety of the Shah, Idi Amin, Bokassa, Somoza, and Gairy, and despite the unmistakable influence they have had on the state and on political forms in their societies, it is not the leaders who determined the character of these states—they are more effect than cause. Consequently, as we shall see, the authoritarian state cannot be reduced to the existence of a dictator or to authoritarian and dictatorial forms of rule, although these accompany it. We must look at the state as a historical materialist category and understand its social and material basis. Further, the nature of the peripheral capitalist state is determined *both* by the internal development of class struggle *and* by the position that these societies, and the classes within them, hold in the global system of capitalism.

There are three further methodological advantages to this approach. One is that the use of concrete examples allows us to study simultaneously the similarities and differences in the form that the state takes in peripheral capitalist societies. We can then avoid two dangers. One is overspecificity—that is, an approach that is premised on the view that since each society is different, there can be no general theories; the other is over-generalization, which results from a preoccupation with similarities. This latter is very common on the left and often leads to the incorrect thesis that since all these states have a broadly common class nature, there is no *real* variety among them. Such an error is not only a matter of theoretical concern, for it can—and has in the past—had a major operational significance. It is similar to the now discredited view that since all developed capitalist societies have a common class content, there is no *real* difference between a bourgeois-democratic state and a fascist state, or between, let us say, the state in Scandinavia and that in Italy or the United States. As Ralph Miliband puts it, this view reveals "an attitude of mind to which Marxists have been prone. This is the belief that because A and B are not *totally* different, they are not *really* different at all. This error has been made in relation to the state, but in other contexts as well, with damaging effects."[11] He then goes on to add:

> There is a permanent Marxist temptation to devalue the distinction between bourgeois-democratic regimes and authoritarian ones. From the view that the former are class regimes of a more or less repressive kind, which is entirely legitimate, it has always been fairly easy for Marxists to move to the inaccurate and dangerous view that what separates them from truly authoritarian regimes is of no great account, or not "qualitatively" significant.[12]

As I shall argue repeatedly in this book, it is vital to make this distinction if the prospects for successful economic, industrial, and political struggles by the workers and peasants in recent postcolonial societies are to be accurately assessed. Yet such struggles all too frequently take place in states that are dominated by military dictatorships or by governments subject to one-party (and often one-person) rule, and these governments are touted by those who wield state power (and even by those who study them) as being democracies or socialist or capitalist.

A further advantage of my approach is that in many parts of the formerly British postcolonial world—and here the Caribbean is a particularly good example—it is widely believed that because of the near total Anglicization of the area, and its relatively recent decolonization, the virtues of "Westminster-type parliamentary democracy" are deeply ingrained in the culture, and that repression, state violence, and dictatorial political rule are therefore unlikely. These are portrayed as a "Latin phenomenon" in the New World, and crudely correlated with "backward" coffee and banana republics. Until recently this belief was widespread among both the ruling class and the dominated majority in these countries. In the Caribbean, the sobering experiences of Eric Gairy's regime in Grenada, Patrick John's in Dominica, and Forbes Burnham's in Guyana have led to a qualified retreat from such simplistic illusions. But this has not been accompanied by any real comprehension of why these developments have taken place, or of the role of subjective and objective factors in their creation and resolution. These regimes are instead treated as deviations from the norm, encouraged by dictatorially inclined political leaders.

It should be borne in mind that while the supposed strength of the democratic tradition in these countries is attributed to British cultural influence, it is presumed to have been aided by the fact that, since the indigenous communities have been virtually annihilated, the British were given a "clean slate," and by the fact that these societies were founded on immigrants from all parts of the globe. While this cultural arrogance is completely misplaced, the fact that these societies are "new" does, as we noted earlier, help us trace the origins of the colonial state more clearly than might be possible elsewhere.

The noncapitalist path as a theory of the state

The only consistently developed body of analysis and practice that deals with the recent postcolonial states is the noncapitalist thesis put forward by the Soviet bloc. As this material is not widely discussed in the English language, I will look at it briefly here so that we can bear in mind the directions in which such an analysis takes us.

What, in essence, does the theory of noncapitalist development argue? It assumes that in precapitalist societies (1) the underdevelopment of the national bourgeoisie and the domination of production by foreign capital means that there is no objective basis for a genuine bourgeois party; that (2) the underdevelopment of industry and manufacturing (as reflected in their small overall share of national production, in the concentration of the industrial workforce in one or two enterprises, and in the amount of widely dispersed small-scale industrial production) means that there is no significant working class and hence no objective basis for a genuine workers' party; that (3) the predominant role of peasants, landowners, the petty bourgeoisie and other intermediate strata, and the unemployed and other nonproletarian strata (which is a reflection of (1) and (2)) creates a particular internal context that favors the leading role played by the petty bourgeoisie and other intermediate strata in the state machinery; and (4) the fact that the balance of world forces is in favor of socialism and national liberation creates a special external context that favors the creation of alternative economic, strategic, and international political relations, and the strengthening of national sovereignty.

The theory argues that since in these societies the petty bourgeoisie and intermediate strata usually dominate the state machinery and political life, and since they hold an objectively intermediate position, they are able to orient the state and politics in a progressive direction—either on the path to non-capitalist and socialist development or in a capitalist direction. To achieve the former, however, certain objective tasks must be pursued. These include (1) building a broad alliance of progressive forces, which may, and often must, include "progressive nationalist" sections of the emerging bourgeoisie; (2) curtailing the dominant role of foreign monopolies in the national economy, usually by way of nationalization and the subsequent creation of a state property sector in the national economy; (3) implementing agrarian reform and pursuing the elimination of all forms of rural exploitation; (4) curtailing domestic monopolies and other such domestic forms of exploitation; (5) creating planning machinery in order to pursue the development of a national industrial sector and diversify the agricultural base of the economy, and to organize the use of state property; (6) pursuing an "independent," "nonaligned," "anti-imperialist" foreign policy; and (7) ensuring the democratization of all aspects of social life and fighting resolutely against dictatorial and antipopular rule. According to the theory, if these tasks are pursued there is no need for capitalism to be established before the transition to socialism is begun. There need be, in other words, no effort to establish a capitalist mode of production. However, the proponents of the noncapitalist thesis reject the assertion that is often made by the leadership in these countries that their societies are socialist, or on the path toward the transition to socialism. Instead they describe them as "national democracies." In addition, they reject the belief that a Marxist or workers' party must control the state and lead social development at every stage after decolonization in order to ensure a progressive noncapitalist path. Indeed, they argue further that a premature assertion of Marxist control of the state power may in fact generate *reversals* for the progressive movement.

How do we evaluate this thesis in light of our project here? I have already dealt with the theory of noncapitalist development at length elsewhere,[13] and want to focus on its relevance for this study. First, however, it should be noted in the thesis's favor that it explicitly distinguishes between what it describes as progressive and nonprogressive states, despite the similarities it recognizes among them. Further, in defining a stage as noncapitalist, and hence distinct from the transition to socialism (and in contradistinction to a pro-capitalist stage), the theory allows for a phase of struggle that is anti-imperialist and oriented against capitalism (and is also antifeudal where appropriate), a phase that is distinct and separate from the transition to socialism. It is a sad commentary on Marxist theoretical works on the state in the "West" that these two issues have not been confronted.

These two issues apart, there are a number of major weaknesses in this theoretical construct. To begin with, the democratization of social life is almost totally ignored, even though it is listed as one of the *objective* tenets that must be pursued. It is assumed that the struggle against imperialism will automatically be democratic and that the pursuit of bourgeois-democratic norms and practices can take a secondary position. As we shall see, this view is both theoretically and operationally incorrect. Worse, within it lie the seeds of the rationalization of dictatorial and authoritarian rule. Second, proponents of the theory overemphasize the significance of foreign policy (and, in particular, positions on nonalignment, African liberation, and the New International Economic Order) and of nationalization as tasks to be pursued. Indeed, the size of the state sector is often taken as an indication of the strength of socialist forces within the state. Third, and following on these two points, the thesis insufficiently emphasizes class struggle *within* these countries. It assumes that because the major classes in these societies are not yet fully developed, class struggles are less intense. It thus fails to grasp the deep complexity and fluidity of class structures in the periphery, particularly where these features are associated with the growth of the state. I shall return to an examination of these features in chapter 5. Arising from this is a fourth consideration: that there is always a disjuncture between state, party, and working-class interests in a given situation. Thus, for instance, the need to protect the interests of the Soviet state may run counter to the interests of "proletarian internationalism." Finally, despite the effort to achieve a balance between theory and practice, the general and the particular, the proponents of this theory nevertheless conduct the debate at the global level of imperialism vs. socialism and separate the analysis from the internal dynamics of class development and class struggle in the peripheral capitalist societies themselves. Many of the regimes described as being on a noncapitalist path are guilty of gross violations of democratic practice, even including the proscription and delegalization of Marxist and communist parties, along with other progressive opposition groups. The countries that are on the list of noncapitalist states is thus bewildering, reflecting the lack of concern about the state of internal class struggle, and states even remain as regimes come and go. Hence Egypt, Ghana, Zambia, Indonesia, Guyana, Afghanistan, Burma, South Yemen, and many more are said to be on the noncapitalist path.

In summary, therefore, our project is essential because the thesis of the noncapitalist path does not provide an adequate theory of the state in the periphery. While it does seek to identify and conceptualize regularities and differences, and while it does attempt to put the role and nature of the state in the period after decolonization and before the "transition to socialism" on the agenda, it fails in other ways. From the standpoint of taking a *political position*, it is crucial to be clear as to what the political interpretation of a progressive national democracy on the noncapitalist path represents *in practice*. As Marx has shown, the bourgeoisie of his day was objectively progressive in relation to its feudal and other precapitalist predecessors. This may be equally the case with the petty bourgeoisie and other intermediate strata who control state power during decolonization. Marx was not, however, led to side with the bourgeoisie! Instead he struggled against it as best as he could. Why? Simply because he recognized the distinction between the objective social advance that a class may represent and the political responsibilities of those committed to ending *all* forms of exploitation and class rule. This meant siding with the class or classes that would make this possible in the long run. And this must be the case with the peripheral capitalist societies as well. Incipient as their various working classes may be, they nevertheless contain the seeds of the future transformation of our world.

Part 1
The Colonial State System

This part of the study is essentially introductory. In it I will trace the impact of colonialism on the formation of the state and on the development of political relations in peripheral societies. As indicated in the discussion on method, I will be drawing mainly on the experiences of the English-speaking Caribbean, but will frequently draw comparisons with other regions in an effort to highlight significant points. The analysis is subdivided into four historical periods, which are meant more as broad indicators of significant changes than as hard-and-fast divisions. I begin with the first phase of European colonization, from the period after the conquest and initial settlement of the "New World," following Columbus's "discovery" in 1492, to the break-up of the slave system in the 1830s. The second period is the period of transition from the abolition of slavery to the era of "free" labor—when a labor market was firmly established—in the early twentieth century. The third period coincides with that of classical imperialism and takes us up to World War II. The final period covers the immediate pre-independence years. Very little historical detail is attempted here. The stress is on the dominant social forces that have shaped the development of the state. Without understanding these, both the importance of the "postcolonial" period and the emergence of the authoritarian state cannot be fully understood.

1. Colonialism, Slavery, and the Emergence of the State

This chapter covers the first historical period, from the conquest and settlement of the "New World" to the break-up of the slave system in the 1830s, and seeks to trace the impact of colonialism and slavery on the state. This period witnessed the effective elimination of the indigenous societies and the creation of immigrant-based slave ones, and so it is useful to start our inquiry with an outline of the major features of the Marxist interpretation of how the state emerged. This will aid our understanding of the process of state emergence in the "New World," where the genocide practiced by the conquering colonial armies created a clean slate on which to write the events that followed.

Marxists see the available anthropological data as suggesting that from the beginning human societies have had certain communal functions that have been performed for the benefit of all through some "organizing authority"—such functions as the resolution of disputes, the organizing of production within the community (when to commence the hunt, where to hunt, etc.), the defense of the community, and so on. This "organizing authority" has taken a variety of social forms, reflecting specific historical, cultural, and environmental conditions. It is also agreed that some form of coercion has always existed in all human societies. This has ranged from extreme forms of coercion imposed by nature, through the economic coercion imposed by the need to provide food, shelter, and clothing in order for family, self, or community to survive, to the conscious "forcible coercion" that a society exercises over individuals and groups and that, as Hal Draper points out, is "usually in the form of an implied last resort, not necessarily an immediate act

3

of force. . . . it is not in the least a question of how often force is actually used, as long as the threat that it can and will be used if necessary is a factor in gaining compliance."[1]

Because Marxists interpret social reality in historical materialist categories, they argue that at a certain stage in the development of the division of labor, exchange, private (as distinct from social/communal) ownership of the factors of production, and the formation of classes, the political organization of society emerges, and that as this happens the social character of these functions, as well as the nature of the exercise of "forcible coercion," are transformed. In other words, the increasing differentiation of productive activities and the emergence of classes are accompanied by new forms of social relations that can be characterized as political and legal. Among these political and legal relations, those that center on the state as an institution are by far the most crucial to the subsequent evolution of class society. Given the key role that classes play after this stage of human development, the political and legal forms of social relations identified here—and indeed the state as an institution (reflecting as well as incorporating these)— would have been unknown in previous nonclass societies, even though organizing authorities clearly existed.

The most important distinguishing feature of the state is therefore that it is a special institution, organized along the lines of a "public power," and has the capacity to impose sanctions if and when necessary. The clearest manifestation of this capacity is the creation of specialized institutions of coercion (army, militia, police, etc.) that are separated from the general body of the society. This feature of the state distinguishes it from the various organizational forms of coercive power that existed in preclass societies. In addition, the coercive power now embodied in this new social form is generally exercised on behalf of the dominant class; this again contrasts with coercive power in preclass societies, which was generally exercised on behalf of the whole society. In this new stage, therefore, coercive power represented in the state becomes *class* power, a power determined and regulated on the basis of private ownership of the factors of production. And from this stage on, coercive power is increasingly exercised *over a given national territory*, as distinct from being exercised over groups of people tied together by blood or kinship.

It is from such a general conception of the historical emergence of the state that Marxists advance the proposition that a key function of the state has been to facilitate the transition from preclass societies (where custom, tradition, habit, and so on were the principal regulators of social relations) to class-structured social systems. Two notes of caution are necessary, however, in interpreting this proposition. One is that just as the development of preclass social formations covered a very long historical period and varied from one society to another, so too the transition to class-structured social systems has covered a long historical period and has varied from one society to another. The proposition, therefore, is necessarily a summary of what has in fact been a long and varied period of human development. The second caution is that because the state is historically rooted in, and develops (albeit at varying pace) out of, those indispensable community functions that were performed even in preclass societies (but that became more and more class determined and regulated during the long transition to class-structured social systems), it is incorrect to treat the state as being the instant invention of a particular class that may, in one way or another, have gained the upper hand and is determined to keep it.

During the long period of transition to class-structured societies, the state sometimes seems to stand above—or at least apart from—society, while imposing its particular forms of class regulation on social relations. As the principal basis of social regulation becomes less and less based on social/communal ownership of the factors of production and more and more on the material interests of the economically dominant class or group, the state becomes increasingly alienated from society while still being an organic part of it. The state, which is organized principally to ensure the new class forms of social regulation, must, to be successful, embrace a number of functions, including several developed previously. Principal among the functions of any state are: (1) Ensuring the protection of the forms of property that the ruling class represents; (2) ensuring that the oppressed classes are held down and do not achieve any reversal in the relations of dominant-dominated; (3) regulating relations between members of the ruling class, and, through this mediation, engendering as much unity as possible in order to protect the fundamental interests of the class; (4) regulating relations between all the propertied classes, including those that are not the ruling class, in order to harmonize the common interests of private property; (5) raising and dispensing of resources within the society; (6) intervening in the process of economic development in order to ensure patterns of accumulation consistent with the class structure of society; (7) creating a bureaucracy to put into effect the laws and regulations that it introduces; (8) training and educating members of the community so as to ensure the reproduction of the labor force and its citizens; (9) intervening in the cultural and ideological arenas in order to ensure developments harmonious with the class structure of the society; (10) protecting the sovereignty of the territory over which it exercises power; and (11) creating the specialized instruments, institutions, and training required to command an effective coercive force without which there can be no guarantee that its other functions will be performed.

It is through the performance of these functions that the various arms of the state—government, administration (in the widest sense of the term), judiciary, security, subcentral government, and the legislature—develop and consolidate themselves.

There are three aspects of the relation of the emerging state to society that have been vital to the effective performance of the above functions. One is that the state necessarily develops within a definite set of social relations in which the production and reproduction of the means of livelihood of the society take place. The state must therefore be analyzed in the context of the structural relations of a particular mode of production, i.e., feudalism, capitalism, slavery, the "Asiatic" mode, and so on. Unless this is done, there is the danger that the category "state" will be reduced to a mere political instrument, that is, to an ideological relation that is derived solely from the consciousness of the people and has no determinate roots in the material basis of social life. In Marxist thought, although ideological relations are treated as essentially "superstructural," they are nevertheless seen as developing out of the material relations of society—those relations that exist among people in the process of producing the material needs of society, and without which social life cannot exist. While these material relations exist independent of the social consciousness of the people, and while it is out of these relations that the state develops, this should not lead to the assumption of any kind of mechanical relation between the material "base" and the state as "super-structure." There is instead a dialectical relation between the development of the state and the material relations of society, and because of this the state has been able at times to operate "relatively independent" of the existing material conditions of social reproduction—that is, to take actions which may directly influence its material "base" or pursue activities beyond what appears to be necessary to ensure the expanded reproduction of the "base." The significance of this point will be taken up more fully in chapter 6.

Second, while in order to be effective the state must possess an effective monopoly of physical force, it also constantly inter-venes in other spheres of social life (for instance, the cultural and ideological spheres mentioned earlier) in order to reduce the need to use its coercive power directly. In other words, those who control the state have always sought, through cul-tural and political intervention, to win "consent" for the ongo-ing system of domination and social reproduction. Thus, while the state must possess a monopoly of physical force as a first requirement, this force is often most effective as a threat and when resorted to only in the last instance. This point is dis-cussed more fully in chapter 8.

Third, although the state emerges as a class institution, it does not end up being a simple, or automatic, instrument of the ruling class. There are a number of reasons for this. One is that the class origins of the personnel of the state may not be the same as that of the ruling class. Another is that the ruling class itself is not usually homogenous, but has contending factions, so that there is no simple determination of the general interest of the ruling class. Furthermore, the state still has to mediate between the ruling class and other classes. These considerations mean that there are great social pressures to make the state relatively independent of the ruling class, *even where the ruling class is relatively homogeneous.* Again, this point will be more fully discussed in chapter 6.

Foundations: colonialism and slavery

In Latin America, and even more so in the Caribbean (and in contrast to Asia and Africa, with their long-settled communities), the foundations of the modern state lie almost exclusively in the historical process in which these territories were incorporated into the European colonial empires. To varying degrees, the process of colonization was accompanied by the elimination of indigenous social forms, the genocide of the indigenous inhabitants, and their replacement by immigrants from Europe, Africa, and Asia, all under European social and political domination.

The first significant European contact with the "New World" came in the form of rudimentary trading outposts that organized exchanges with the indigenous inhabitants. The principal products acquired were precious stones and metals, spices (pepper, ginger, mace, cloves), woven artifacts, stoneware, and so on. Islands were occupied and accessible ports were established, either on the coasts or up-river in the mainland territories. During this period merchant capitalist forms predominated in Europe and the approach to colonization was to appropriate surplus value through the purchase of finished products at "prices" below their "values." During this period little or no account was taken of the conditions of production of these commodities. This type of colonization differed from that of the ancient Egyptian and Roman empires, the Aztec and Incan empires of the New World itself, and even from the Ottoman empire of the sixteenth and seventeenth centuries, where the simple pillage of territory gave way to various forms of exacting tribute from available surpluses (both foodstuffs and luxury goods) for consumption in the imperial centers and to the eventual capture of people and the exaction of forced labor for the benefit of the conquerors. In the colonies we are discussing, on the other hand, trading posts and the simple mercantil-

ist appropriation of surpluses were superceded by more organized settlements as the European colonists moved inland and
sought to exploit the land themselves—and in the process imposed their own forms of control over the conditions of production. As indicated earlier, this required the defeat and virtual
extinction of the original inhabitants in order to facilitate the
seizing of their territory. Nowhere in the New World was the
labor supplied by the surviving indigenous communities
enough for the task of settling and exploiting the land and
resources. Nor could the migrants who came from Europe
(principally poor whites brought out as indentured servants,
convicts, and early small settlers) supply enough labor. The
result was that the Europeans proceeded forcibly to import the
peoples of Africa: thus was the barbarous slave trade born.
Recourse to slavery during this period did not happen
everywhere, but was influenced by a variety of factors, such as
climate, "accidents" of history, the policies of the colonizing
power, the state of colonial rivalries, and so on.

While there can be no gainsaying the fact that the indigenous
peoples had stoutly resisted the genocidal policies of the col-
onizers and the seizure of their land, the superiority of European firepower, organization, and economic resources prevailed. Where indigenous communities did survive, it was
because they were driven into isolated areas, thus becoming
marginalized (as in Guyana), or were brought into the service of
the European-dominated economies (as in Colombia, Mexico,
and Guatemala). By the early seventeenth century, African
slave labor dominated the Caribbean workforce and exported,
plantation-produced tropical staples had become the main
form of economic activity, replacing the earlier exchange of
treasure. The pattern of settlement differed from that of the
northern colonies on the mainland, which was based on a
more-or-less self-sufficient and diversified small-farmer economy, and from the hacienda of Central and South America,
which appeared similar but was self-sufficient and was also
more feudal in its social structure than the plantation.

The plantation was the principal institutional/organizational
form through which European settlement was effected in the
Caribbean. The typical plantation was based on a rigid hierar-

chy of class and race, in which the work process was directed by extremely authoritarian and brutal forms of social control. At the apex of this hierarchy was the white planter; at the base was the African slave laborer. While the plantation has been called a "total" institution because it undertook the entire range of administrative and authority functions, this was certainly not true in the sense that the plantation was a determinate mode of production. It was simply an institution—albeit one with immensely far-reaching social significance—but it was itself rooted in a particular mode of production, what I have elsewhere called the "colonial slave mode of production."[2] Alongside the plantation there existed a small number of petty commodity producers made up of "free" people—white and nonwhite—as well as isolated areas of natural economy among the indigenous Amerindian inhabitants; these did not constitute separate modes of production, however, but spheres of social activity maintained for the purpose of ensuring *and* subsidizing the reproduction of the slave workforce, which made up the overwhelming majority of direct producers.

The slave status of the workforce made possible what can be called the "extra-economic" appropriation of the surplus, and determined the dominant form of the relations of exploitation in the economic structure of the society. Consequently, even though the slaves produced commodities for exchange on the world market (sugar, cotton, indigo), as the direct producers they were not themselves subject to commodity relations and were not part of a labor market. This slave status meant that the mode of production was *clearly determined by the colonizing power*, and was in no way a "natural" outgrowth of the development of the indigenous communities in the New World. Consequently, slavery did not take the classic form which evolved in Europe, where it was the direct outgrowth of the internal dissolution of communalism and on the exaction of tribute and plunder among warring communities. And while the plantations often operated as "little states," the planters always recognized two major limitations on their power. First, in view of the numerical disparity between masters and slaves, masters could not rely exclusively on their own resources for policing the slaves, except if this was limited to "minor" insurrections. For more general insurrections, supplemental aid from other planters and the colonial power itself was essential. In addition, in the face of continuous colonial rivalries and wars, the forces of the ruling metropolitan power had to be relied upon to protect the colonial territory as a whole. It should be remembered that this was the period when the newer powers, such as Britain, France, Holland, and Denmark, were challenging the imperial hegemony of Portugal and Spain, and, as a result, colonial conflict was increasing and colonies changed hands frequently.

The second limitation was that the requirements of agricultural production and trade necessitated the development of certain organizing functions on the part of the state—the construction of ports, for instance—and these increased over time. Even those activities which fell within the planters' purview—health, education, roads, etc.—were overseen by the local governor, appointed by the colonial power. Thus although the state was indeed a very underdeveloped institution during this period, the plantation was not by any means a "total institution."[3]

The colonial context not only determined the slave status of the direct producers, but colonialism was the structure through which the influences of emerging capitalism in Europe were transmitted to the region. (It is termed *emerging* capitalism because the period of consolidation of the colonial slave mode of production in the Caribbean broadly coincided with the transition from the era of merchant capital in Europe, and the creation of a world market, to the era of industrial capitalism and the altered patterns of world economic relations this generated.) The colonial mediation of emerging European capitalism constitutes an aspect of the colonial slave mode of production which has had far-reaching significance for the postcolonial period, as several Caribbean examples will illustrate.

A first example is that while the plantations were in the main oriented toward production of tropical staples for profit, and while this profit was privately appropriated, there were important variations to this process. Thus, in the case of sugar production, despite heavy investment in overhead for factories, field preparation, water control systems, storage and transportation, and slaves, the outlook among sugar planters was largely speculative, in keeping with the general undeveloped character of merchant capital at that time and reinforced by the fact that the prices of tropical export staples, and in particular sugar, were very uncertain because of competition from other producers and in spite of protective tariffs. Furthermore, many of the early planters originated from the landed classes in Britain and linked their economic speculation in the colonies to their social status at "home." Successful planters therefore used the surpluses generated locally to buy peerages and estates back home, either to reinforce their status there or to gain entry into the landed gentry. In this way colonially produced surplus was "consumed" elsewhere, rather than being plowed back into the plantation, and did not become the same driving force in expanding value that accumulation became in capitalist societies at the center. In this respect, therefore, the colonial slave mode was in many ways not capitalist but precapitalist in essence.

This orientation toward speculative profit, used in part for consumption back home, was also reflected in certain precapitalist patterns of local investment and technology. When expanding output, the planters more often than not emphasized the extensive, rather than the intensive, exploitation of labor, so that instead of seeking to raise productivity per worker hour, the emphasis was on longer working hours for the existing slaves or on the acquisition of additional slaves. It was only because slaves could generally be bought and kept cheaply that such an approach was feasible and profitable. The land was also extensively, rather than intensively, exploited. Thus adding new acreage rather than instituting new and better farming practices accounted for most of the increases in output attributable to land. Further, the extensive use of both land and capital (slaves) was accompanied by a very low level of development and application of technology. This was combined, however, with a high degree of specificity of capital equipment, so that the layout of the canefields prevented their easy adaptation to other crops, and sugar factories could not be converted to other purposes.

The principal effect of the colonial mediation of capitalist development in Europe was that agricultural production—

indeed all the major economic activities—in the colonies was oriented toward servicing, at a profit, the needs of the colonizing power. A list of principal agricultural crops produced in the plantations even before sugar became dominant testifies to this orientation: they included cacao, coffee, tobacco, indigo, coconuts—every one destined for export. The colonies were developing a structure of output in which what was produced domestically was exported, while what was consumed was imported. Further, as long as the colonial slave mode of production was in ascendancy, the plantation remained the dominant institution and the colonial office was all-powerful, so that the local territorial state could only develop very slowly.

The links between European capital expansion and the local planter class was therefore concretely expressed in the link between tropical production and the consumption requirements of the European masses (rather than in the needs of the inhabitants of the exporting societies), and in the links between the local planter class and the merchant and landed classes in Europe. It was only to be expected that in these circumstances the ownership and management structure of the plantation would reflect the forces at work in the colonial slave mode of production as a whole. At first the plantations were owned and controlled by resident planters, but by the time of the abolition of slavery in the 1830s, the owners were largely absentee landlords who relied on managerial staff recruited in Europe and sent out on contract to run the estates. As we shall see in succeeding chapters, once back home many of the absentee owners became intimately linked to the development of capitalism in Europe, developing economic interests that were directly or indirectly connected with the colonial trade—shipping, the procurement of supplies—and these connections were to play a vital role in the eventual diversification of the plantation. In addition, the growth of absentee proprietorship reduced the patriarchal tendencies within the plantation and eased the transition from slavery to the modern forms of dependency that prevail today.

Under the impetus of industrial development in Europe, the surplus that was initially plowed back into consumption gradually began to fuel the requirements of industrial capitalism instead, and its extraction from the colonies became more systematic. Again, it was clearly colonial mediation, particularly through the support of the colonial state and the European finance houses, that made it possible to drain the surplus out of the colonies in an organized fashion. This was crucial to the later development of these societies, for it meant that the colonial slave mode of production, oriented as it was toward servicing the needs of European capital expansion, could not develop a strong enough internal momentum to ensure that its surpluses were used for the development of an indigenous capitalism.

In the light of the above, Banaji's observation is apt: one cannot simply equate the establishment of a world market dominated by a rapidly expanding Europe with the installation of capitalist modes of production in the colonies.[4] The colonial mediation referred to here should not be reduced to the notion that capitalism was transplanted into the colonies, or to the belief that the economic structure of the colonies was determined by the "world market" that developed along with capitalism. Although the colonial slave mode was indeed organically linked to the process of capitalist expansion in Europe, it took root under specific conditions of environment and culture, one in which African slaves and European masters were locked in deadly antagonism.

Colonial slavery and the state: an assessment

What important conclusions can be drawn for a theory of the state in the periphery from this period of colonial slavery in the New World? To begin with, in all colonies the process of colonization ultimately required the effective concentration of power in the hands of the colonizing power. Where, in the process of colonization, more-or-less strong and stable indigenous authorities and organizing institutions are encountered— chieftaincies, tribal structures, local suzerainties, regulated local laws, etc.—as was the case in India and coastal Africa, the colonial power is forced either to eliminate, manipulate, or neutralize these or to pursue some combination of these approaches in order to ensure its own domination. The first conclusion is, therefore, that in the last resort dual bases of state power cannot exist in the territories under colonial rule. State power flows from the authority of the colonial power downward, no matter what local challenges it faces. If indigenous sources of state power are to prevail, the colonial authority must first be destroyed.

A second conclusion is that, as I argued in the previous section, in circumstances such as those in the Caribbean, where indigenous political institutions were undeveloped and where the natural economy and various forms of communalism were destroyed by the colonial power, the origins of the colonial state are to be found in the process of colonization itself. Third, despite the widely proclaimed "totality" of the private plantation, the local state, no matter how rudimentary its level of development, nevertheless developed as a separate institutional form within the colonial slave mode of production. This was possible because there were functions which, because of their private ownership and control, the plantations could not perform effectively. Such functions required a separate *public power* which developed organically within the local state. This process gained momentum as colonial societies became increasingly complex, and as contradictions and conflicts emerged among the major social groups: planters, slaves, "free" whites and nonwhites, merchants, traders, and public officials representing the local state and the Colonial Office. The Colonial Office became less and less inclined to intervene in day-to-day matters and increasingly relied on the local state to represent its interests. This was encouraged by the planters, who, although invariably loyal to the "Crown," nevertheless felt themselves to be the best judges of local circumstances.

Of course, even though the local state developed out of the need for an organizing authority to perform certain "common" functions in the local society and the need to have an "on-the-spot" public coercive power to guarantee the interests of the dominant local and colonial interests, it did so in the context of a colonial power exercising ultimate control over, and responsibility for, the territory. The overarching presence of the colonial power is a common feature in all colonial societies, no matter what form colonization takes. As a consequence, the local state has always had to develop under colonial tutelage, so that from its inception it has been the representative of the dominant colonial interests. The character of the colonial state can therefore only be fully appreciated in relation *both* to the internal influences on its growth and development, and to this particular external context of its creation and development. It follows that the colonial state is not *either* exclusively or independently determined by internal developments in the colonized territory, or a simple imposition of the colonial power.

The political organization of the society was confined within the immediate framework of the state and restricted to Colonial Office officials and the few planters who ran the state machinery. The absence of political organization in the community at large meant that the local state apparatus was used crudely in the pursuit of the material interests of the colonists and planters.

A fourth conclusion that can be derived from this period of history is that the development of the state facilitated the development of legal forms, but that in order to ensure their effectiveness it was necessary that the "public power," organized through the state, be seen as prevailing over the armed indigenous societies as well as over the ruling class itself, in its various plantation militias. Fifth, further expansion of the state and its functions would rest heavily on the extension of a labor market to the entire workforce. The system of production was based on slavery, so that custom and the whim of the planter, not the market, regulated relations between workers and employers. Until workers became "free" to choose their employers, labor power could be bought and sold; and until workers could begin to organize in defense of their interests, individual plantation regulations would continue to be a substitute for functions that the state would later take on.

Sixth, while in each colony the labor market was limited, the plantations did produce for sale in the international market. Thus the spread of market relations of all types occurred in the context of the brutality of slavery. This legacy, as I shall argue in Part 2, remains an important element in the forms and practices of state power exercised in certain colonies today.

Finally, it is worth repeating a point made earlier: a dual

conception of the colonial state (as both internally and externally determined) must be kept firmly in mind at all stages of the analysis. If we fail to do this, we will fail to appreciate that the colonial state from its beginning embodied both a system of (class) oppression *and* a system of national oppression, neither of which is independent of the other. In this sense, therefore, the colonial state is the *specific* product of a very particular phase of development.

2. Transition: The Emergence of Labor and the Colonial State

The consolidation of the colonial state

In this chapter I will trace the impact of the major developments from emancipation to the turn of the nineteenth century on the colonial state. This period coincided with the intensification of the Industrial Revolution in Western Europe, and the social forces associated with this development tilted the balance against slavery in the colonies, leading to the legal abolition of the slave trade, first by Denmark, then by Britain (in 1807), followed by Holland, Sweden, and France in the 1820s. Slavery itself was subsequently abolished—in British possessions in 1833.

Many developments within the colonies, Western Europe, and the wider world were responsible for the breakdown of slavery. For our purposes, two developments outside the colonies should be emphasized. One was that in Europe during the late eighteenth and early nineteenth centuries the rapidly growing class of industrial capitalists was more interested than their mercantile counterparts had been in finding outlets for their machine-produced products and in finding raw materials (cotton, vegetable oils, dyestuffs, etc.) to import, as well as basic foods for the populations of the growing industrial areas. They were no longer interested in occupying territory in order to capture supplies of precious metals, exotic tropical products, and slaves, or in creating white settler outlets for their own population. As Harry Magdoff has pointed out, these developments required the development of colonial policies that would alter the social structure of the colonies to fit the new purpose.[1] These included overhauling existing land and property arrangements; creating, in place of slaves, a stable labor supply for commercial agriculture and mining; extending the use of money and exchange, frequently by requiring the payment of money taxes and land rent; including a decline in domestic-oriented activities, and, particularly in the case of India and its cotton products, curtailing export production in order to facilitate the export of British goods. These changes in colonial policy required changes in the internal structure of the colonies, and these in turn required new directions in colonial administration, including the encouragement of stable state structures within the colonies. After the break-up of slavery in the 1830s and the immense social changes that this engendered, the colonial state began increasingly to take on the form that lasted until the turn of the century. The influence of these "external" factors in the formation of the state must be understood clearly.

The second aspect of "international" developments that must be emphasized is that by the end of the eighteenth century Spain and Portugal were too weak to sustain their empires, either from the challenges of other colonial powers or from the people they sought to subjugate. The colonies won several victories, so that by 1825 Spain had lost all of its colonies on the South American mainland and held only the islands of Puerto Rico and Cuba, while Brazil had become independent of Portugal. The British Empire, although weakened by the revolt of the American colonies and the growing influence of the United States in the New World, was nevertheless consolidating the gains of its second wave of empire building—in India, in Australia, and in parts of coastal Africa (Sierra Leone, 1808; Gambia, 1816; Gold Coast, 1821). This meant that the end of the slave trade—and of slavery itself—did not signal the end of the idea of empire building. The British simply sought to give a new direction to this process, and it was this that was to influence the way in which Britain encouraged the consolidation of state forms in its colonies.

In the British colonies in the Caribbean the emancipation of the slaves and the emergence of a "free" labor market were stubbornly resisted by the local planter class, and in the end the ruling classes in Britain had to "impose" a solution. But planter resistance was strong enough to delay the emergence of a labor market, and in some territories—Guyana and Trinidad, in particular—the planters succeeded in replacing slavery with a system of indentured immigration in which immigrants from all parts of the world (but mainly from India) were brought to the colonies under "contracts" that provided for a "legally" binding forward sale of their labor. These quasislave conditions were reinforced by the requirement that each immigrant be personally bonded to a particular plantation owner: their contracts forbade them to work for any employer other than the one with whom the contract was signed. The wage rate was set by local law, and the worker was legally bound to perform whatever tasks his "employer" required, six days a week for a five-year period. Unexplained absences were treated as "desertion" and carried severe penalties.

The immediate post-slavery period was therefore one in which the colonial state that had emerged during the slave period had to consolidate itself in the face of the transformation of the status of the workforce from slave to "free" and of the development of an independent peasantry created when the newly freed slaves moved into agricultural self-employment. This was in addition to the adaptations it had to make to the new directions colonial policy was taking because of "external" developments. The state form that emerged was called Crown Colony government. Its basic principles were: (1) Extremely limited electoral rights, used in determining the composition of the local law-making and executive bodies; (2) an overwhelming concentration of authority in the executive branch; and (3) an appointed personal representative of the colonial power—usually the local governor—whose veto power gave him ultimate executive authority.

The typical Crown Colony government was designed to contain all local resistance to colonial interests, and it did so by ensuring a maximum number of authoritarian forms of rule and a minimum amount of control over the organs of the state from below. This type of state structure, with its extremely limited franchise—which ensured that it was comprised entirely of appointed colonial officials and elected planters—was extremely "instrumental," in the sense that the dominant classes ruled directly. There was, in other words, no significant disjuncture between class power and state power. The ruling groups were by-and-large singleminded in their use of the state machinery to buttress their authority and consolidate the dominance of the plantation-based cash-crop economy. When and where they could, they used their power to retard the development of both the "free" labor system and the peasantry. Thus, to take one example, the indentured immigration system lasted until 1921 in Guyana even though Latin America had by then been long independent and the final wave of global colonization had peaked in Africa. Of course, the singlemindedness portrayed here did not rule out conflicts between planters and Colonial Office officials, particularly since the former tended to regard themselves as the experts on the local situation.

Summarizing the main features of the formation of the state during the period between the end of slavery and the beginning of the twentieth century, we see an intensification in the development of certain state functions, one which, although begun in the earlier period, now begins to assume a new significance. The more important of these were:

(1) The police and other "peacekeeping" instruments grew as the state sought to ensure internal stability following the abolition of slavery.

(2) The judicial system expanded to deal with the matters listed below, as well as to adjudicate disputes created by the growth of a money, business, and private-land economy.

(3) Local mechanisms were developed for dealing with the colonial power on matters of trade and commerce in a particular territory—currency circulation, trade preferences, etc. This was important since the commercial needs of the planters were not necessarily regarded as important by the Colonial Office, which was operating from the point of view of the "mother" country and/or the other colonies.

(4) Mechanisms were also developed for ensuring greater control over the land—by taking property, controlling its transfer to the peasantry, facilitating the process of centralizing land in the hands of the landed oligarchy, protecting and controlling the distribution of Crown lands, etc.

(5) A system for administering the indenture and other tied labor systems was developed—laws were passed on such mat-

ters as payment for work, the number of work days per year and hours of work per day, punishments for nonfulfillment of work obligations, etc.

(6) A system for supervising the growth of the labor market was instituted.

(7) A greater interest in education developed, even though education effectively remained the domain of the churches.

(8) And, to finance all of the above, local taxes were raised and import duties imposed.

These functions allowed the local ruling class to intervene in those areas of the state that it wanted to develop in its own interests, and yet at the same time to subscribe to the general ideological outlook of the European ruling classes that the "best government is the least government"—meaning minimal intervention of the state in the private regulation of commodity production and social life, but less parsimony in the development of its coercive arm if circumstances warranted it, or in its support of the centralization of wealth in the hands of the ruling oligarchy.

Depending on local circumstances, the class structure of the state in this period was reinforced by the developing racial structure of the society as a whole. The ruling planter class, its resident representatives, and the representatives of the Colonial Office were white Europeans. The ex-slaves were black Africans, the few remaining indigenous peoples were Amerindians, and the indentured workers—in those territories that had them—came mainly from India, with a significant sprinkling of Chinese and Portuguese. There were also persons of mixed racial descent in all the territories, and they, as well as the ex-slaves, migrated from one territory to another within the Caribbean region. The occupational structure of these economies was markedly stratified by race, and while the principal racial contradiction remained that between the white ruling class and the nonwhite direct producers, manipulation by the white ruling class, combined with prejudice born of ignorance of each other's cultural traditions, resulted in strong ethnic and communal differences among the nonwhite workforce. Racial relations were therefore superimposed on class relations, giving a definite form to the pattern of ideological domination. Notions such as "inherent white supremacy," and the Europeans' "civilizing mission" dominated the ruling class's relationship to the workforce and provided the rationale for the brutal exploitation of nonwhite labor. At the same time, racial ideas about "blacks," "coolies," and "ignorant savages" were deliberately used to divide the workforce of ex-slaves and indentured workers and to isolate the indigenous Indians.

The phase during which the local planter class and colonial officials administered the state machinery did not last indefinitely. It was based on a highly restrictive suffrage, and as an influential strata of local businessmen, merchants, shop-keepers, teachers, professionals, and so on, emerged among the nonwhites, certain nationalist ideas in favor of a wider suffrage and greater participation in government began to emerge. The new groups, in their effort to dilute the hold of Crown Colony government and improve their position within the state, appealed to nationalism and against white racism, albeit in relatively muted terms. They saw participation in the colonial state as a principal means of enhancing their social and economic status within the society, with the result that wherever the elective principal had been established a struggle ensued over elective office. During the period under consideration, however, a highly restricted suffrage prevailed, which worked against the advance of these groups, and they were forced to widen the area of agitation. No longer did they simply petition the local government and the Colonial Office for a more representative local state; now they sought support for an expanded suffrage and more elective offices from among sections of the working class and peasantry, also under the banner of "nationalism."

Theoretical conclusions

Certain points emerge from the foregoing that are of significance to our inquiry into the development of state and society. First, while the state continued to expand—in part out of its obligation to provide functions which, as we saw in the previous chapter, not even the plantations as so-called total institutions could provide—two aspects of this expansion were particularly important, in keeping as they were with the new circumstances. One was the relatively greater development of the coercive and judicial apparatuses of the state as compared to its other aspects, for the fear of disruption following the abolition of slavery was widespread. The second was that all the state functions manifested their class characteristics openly. There was no strategic need to appear to govern "by consent," revealing unmistakably an important characteristic of the form that domination was taking. On the other hand, this pattern of state domination was accompanied by the spread of labor-market relations and the rapid formation of the two classes (workers and peasants) that in this and later periods became the focus of local opposition to colonial and planter class interests. Although trade unions, peasant associations, and other such forms of internal organization did not yet exist, their ability to move freely within the country, and to "freely" withhold their labor and their produce from the market, was a weapon to be feared. Nevertheless, the ruling class continued to be firmly in control of the structure of production and the key positions within the state machinery were all held by colonial officials or the plantocracy. And the plantocracy itself, with growing links to the ruling class in Europe, facilitated the integration of local resource use into metropolitan needs, thereby helping to perpetuate its reign. Thus while these developments favored the local ruling classes vis-à-vis their class enemies (the emerging labor force and peasantry, formed out of the newly freed slaves, and the newly arrived indentured immigrants), its dominant position within the state structure stemmed from its economic power and control of resources. In other words, the *political* power of the dominant classes flowed from their *economic* power and not vice-versa. As I shall argue in Part 2, the situation was reversed in the postcolonial period.

Third, with the end of slavery colonial society became increasingly complex, particularly in the spread of commodity relations. It was this development that gave birth to the intermediate strata—merchants, professionals, craftsmen, etc.—

referred to earlier. As the demand for greater local rule and a wider franchise was taken up by these sections of the population, the period was marked by both advances and retrogressions in constitutional development within the colonies.

In the colonies, the colonial power responded to the increasing pressure for a greater local voice by widening the franchise. Nevertheless, in the evolution of the colonial state structure as a whole, the executive power (because of the position of the governor and the Colonial Office) remained much stronger than the legislative power. And, despite the links between the local and metropolitan ruling classes, there were regular conflicts with the Colonial Office, particularly over taxation and trade policies. Indeed, as we saw, abolition itself had to be imposed by the Colonial Office over the wishes of the planters. The industrial bourgeoisie in Britain favored free trade in the international market; the local planters, however, threatened by competition from other colonies that produced cane sugar, as well as by beet sugar production in Europe, were in favor of protection and of special colonial trade relations. While in the United States and some parts of the Caribbean and Latin America such conflicts eventually led to open revolt and national independence for the colonies, in the English, French, and Dutch-speaking Caribbean this did not happen, perhaps because of the racial composition of these societies. Ultimately, fear of the nonwhite masses (itself a result of the ideology used to justify white rule) forced the effort to resolve conflicts within the context of an assured presence of the colonial power.

Fifth, as we observed earlier, at the ideological level the development of local state functions, events notwithstanding, was influenced by the laissez-faire, noninterventionist ideology of the period, which emanated from the metropole. Acceptance of such an ideology by the local ruling class did not, however, prevent it from intervening against the workers and peasants, or from pursuing its own interests. Nor did it prevent the development of racism as an aspect of ideological relations, which was to play an enduring role in the organization of the state in these colonies.

Finally, therefore, and in a sense in summary of these points, we must always keep in mind that the process of consolidation of the colonial state in this period had two key aspects, internal and external. And while the focus is often on the internal—on the nature of the emerging classes, for instance—we make a serious mistake if we neglect the colonial context in which the consolidation was taking place.[2]

3. The Emergence of Peripheral Capitalism and the Colonial State

Imperialism and peripheral capitalism

So far I have considered the main contours of the development of the colonial state in two historical periods, from its emergence during the colonial slave mode of production to its consolidation during the subsequent period of transition to "free" labor in the late nineteenth century. In this chapter I consider the third period of colonialism, from the turn of the century up until World War II. It should be remembered that during the second period the ruling planter class used its economic and political power to try and stem the development of a "free" labor force and labor market, as well as the development of domestic agriculture and its associated peasantry. These efforts failed, however, not only because they were resisted by the dominated classes within the colonial society, but also because they ran counter to momentous transformations under way in Europe. These transformations continued well into the period under consideration, reaching and affecting every sphere of social life. The most important effect of this from our point of view was the emergence of a group of countries that has been described as the "center" of the world capitalist system (principally in Europe and America) and another group, comprising most of the rest of the world, which became a "periphery." By the turn of the century the capitalist system had matured into its classic (Leninist) imperialist phase. These changes necessarily affected—and in turn were affected by—the development of the state in the colonial and ex-colonial possessions. This chapter will survey some of the key features of these developments as they affected the colonial state.

The fundamental feature of this period is that by its end the slave-based mode of colonial exploitation, which had developed out of the first modern wave of empire building, had given way to other forms of economic structure and colonial power–colony relations associated with the development of central and peripheral capitalism. Britain, which remained the leading capitalist country and colonial power, had by the early twentieth century consolidated its monopolistic industrial structure. In addition, the peasantry was entirely proletarianized; an industrial working class, accompanied by the growth of large-scale worker organizations, was established; the tenacious hold of the landed gentry on the political system and the state had been broken; and political power and the state apparatus were firmly in the hands of the economically dominant bourgeoisie. In terms of external economic relations, the Leninist form of Britain's imperialist relations was manifested in a rapid growth in the export of capital to finance the development and export of primary agricultural and mineral produce from the colonies for use in industry and for mass consumption in Britain. The increasing tendency toward monopoly, combined with the emphasis on the export of capital, provided the social basis for the emergence of the post-World War II oligopolistic transnational corporate structure.

The move to this type of transnational structure meant a shift in emphasis to deriving profits from direct and indirect control of foreign resources and markets, and it had the paradoxical effect of strengthening nationalist tendencies, both in the center and the periphery. In the period before World War II, the leading capitalist countries all saw strong surges of nationalistic fervor. Combined with the competitive struggle for markets, resources, and territory, this occasioned many vicious commercial and political rivalries, which in turn led to a series of major conflagrations and wars—the most devastating being World War I and World War II. An important result was that by the end of World War II the role of the state in the center countries was greatly enhanced. This was dramatically exhibited in the increased scope and complexity of the internal regulation of their economies, and in the extent to which state power became the main promoter of the imperialist designs of the national ruling classes.

No society—let alone those that remained direct colonial appendages of the metropolitan powers—was able to withstand these transformations. Indeed, this period saw a new wave of colonial expansion, including the scramble for colonial possessions in Africa, even though the earlier colonial empires in Latin America had been dismembered and the United States, an ex-colony, was on the verge of becoming the leading capitalist nation.

The peripheral capitalist social formation that had emerged had a number of specific characteristics. First, and most obviously, many countries had been *politically dominated* by a few. All of Latin America, the Caribbean, Africa, and Asia—with the exception of Japan—had come under one form or other of colonial rule (from gunboat diplomacy to unequal treaties to protectorates to the Crown Colony system of colonies proper), and had suffered it for periods ranging from a few decades to several centuries.

Second, the capitalist center countries *economically dominated* all but a few of the politically independent countries, as well as the colonial possessions. Both groups of countries had developed as colonies, and their patterns of resource use, production, exchange, consumption, and class relations had been, and continued to be, mediated through colonial domination. The result, as we saw earlier, was that in these societies the "self-centered" autonomous development of productive factors had been curtailed, resource use had been blocked, and precapitalist relations had been preserved in certain areas, particularly agriculture. The key consideration had been to ensure that those areas of commodity production needed to service the metropolitan power were "free" so that they could be organized to satisfy these needs.

Third, the system of domination that emerged was based on an imperialist-imposed international division of labor and an internal class structure and pattern of social relations in which the reproduction of the system of domination was the predominant, but not exclusive, purpose. It is important to note, however, that the relation of the peripheral countries to the capitalist centers was not mechanistic or deterministic. There was often a relative independence or autonomy in these relations;

this could be clearly seen at times of war and intense rivalry among the imperial powers, or when local or international developments propelled nationalist sentiments to the fore, not only among the masses, but among the local ruling classes as well.

By the end of the period under consideration, then, the world capitalist system had two clear sections, the central capitalist formations and the peripheral capitalist formations. While the development of both responded to the demands of the reproduction and expansion of capitalist relations on a world scale, in the central capitalist formations this process came to be known as "development," while in the peripheral capitalist formations it came to be known as "underdevelopment." The latter was defined as the perpetuation of distorted economic structures, which could be seen in the underdevelopment of industry (both extensively and intensively), the limited differentiation of agricultural production, the secondary role of the internal market in determining patterns of resource use, and a pattern of internal consumption that does not reflect the needs of the broad masses of the population. In addition, low levels of indigenous technological development, combined with the import of high-level technology for those sectors most integrated into the developed capitalist economies, created marked disparities in levels of labor productivity that paralleled the different social relations in the two broad sectors of the local economy, with the extensive precapitalist sector usually constituting the major source of both a labor supply and of primitive accumulation. It is in this context that surpluses were systematically drained from the underdeveloped to the developed areas of the capitalist world system.

The final result was the creation of a system in which economic expansion in the underdeveloped social formations of the capitalist system depended upon the expansion of capital in the developed social formations. Autonomous or "self-centered" accumulation was, and remains today, the exception rather than the rule. It is in this context that we must look at the social forces that played a role in the consolidation of the state in the periphery. Again, this is not an attempt to trace historical development in any detail but to provide an interpretive/

analytic outline of the main contours of a historical process in order to inform the analysis and conclusions developed in Part 2.

The transformation of internal social relations

What was the effect of this new phase of imperialist development and internal class struggle on the social structure of the periphery, and how did it affect the development of the colonial state? Class struggle, combined with the global transformation of capitalism (and propelled by developments in the center countries), transformed the structure of these societies in many ways. Among the most crucial changes in the Caribbean were the following: First, the dominant plantation form of organizing economic activity underwent a major transformation. The historical tendency toward the concentration and centralization of land and capital in the sugar industry was accelerated by the prolonged periods of depression and crisis in the late nineteenth and early twentieth centuries and by the effects of the two world wars. Thus in Guyana, for instance, by the end of World War II two transnational firms controlled 90 percent of sugarcane production and *all* the processing facilities. These firms were already somewhat diversified internationally, and locally they were increasingly becoming engaged in activities ancillary to sugar production, such as shopkeeping, coastal and international shipping, foundries, pharmaceuticals, and alcohol production. While the structure of all these local activities continued to be based on the integration of the local ruling class into the ruling class in Britain, the latter was by this time predominantly a manufacturing-oriented bourgeoisie. This influenced the outlook and economic operations of the local ruling class, as can be seen not only in the very process of diversification indicated above, but in two entirely new developments. One was the reduced emphasis on tropical agriculture, and in particular sugar, as "speculative" crops. The available evidence suggests that in this period there was a search for secure, long-term profits in the process of production, aided no doubt by the removal of the grip of the paternalistic planter over the estate. The other development was the increased role of science and technology in the struggle to improve productivity and reduce the cost of sugar manufacture, a process that was already evident in the late nineteenth century but accelerated in the period leading up to World War II.

Second, with the ending of all forms of tied labor, including indenture, and the development of a labor market came new systems of worker-employer relations. Principal among these was the development of trade unions, which began in the early twentieth century. Third, the growth of a labor market brought with it an increasingly high level of open unemployment, which was reinforced by the high rate of natural population increase (which followed improved sanitation, the introduction of better water supply systems, etc.), the progressive mechanization of the plantations, and the ruin of small craftspeople by imports.

Fourth, despite many restrictions the peasantry nevertheless expanded, although even by the end of the period it was still an essentially dependent social group faced with all the difficulties usually encountered by small-scale commodity producers in the context of backward social relations. But, as the peasantry developed, so did its stratification, creating in its wake indigenous forms of exploitation, landlordism, and extensive peasant indebtedness. Despite the agricultural orientation of these economies, the internal market for food was so poorly organized and underdeveloped that few peasants could subsist on agriculture alone. Many men and women were forced to operate as part-time laborers on the estates, or to seek jobs in government public works programs to avoid destitution. And while a definite working class was coming into existence, as were worker organizations, the internal organization of the peasantry was extraordinarily weak. The result was that the peasantry as a social group was poorly placed in the intense economic and social struggles that were to come.

As the economy became more complex and commodity relations spread, a fifth feature of the social structure became prominent. This was the rapid rise in influence of a local class of merchants and traders who dealt in retailing, wholesaling, and the provision of such transport and financial services as banking and insurance. Members of this class were sometimes closely linked to the sugar activities of the plantations, but were often independent of these. While as a class these groups shared common property interests with the economically dominant planter class, ultimately they were excluded from it on racial grounds. And as nationalist pressures for control of the state developed, along with pressures by local political organizations, these groups often found themselves driven into head-on political conflict with the planter class.

Along with these merchant groups there emerged a group of educated local professionals. This group sought to consolidate itself by gaining control of the state apparatus and constituting the corps from which the "local" political elite was drawn. In order to pursue its political interests, this group forged an alliance with the masses and with the other petty bourgeois and intermediate strata in the struggle for constitutional reform. While the objective initially was limited to the demand for greater participation in the colonially structured state system, as the struggle developed the objective was widened, and after World War II it merged into the wider demand for national independence.

The colonial state in the periphery

These developments had a major impact on the colonial state. First, those who controlled the local state were forced to abandon their laissez-faire ideology and to encourage the state to play an increasingly active part in providing the basis for a "modern" economy. This period thus saw the role of the state as an institution of economic reproduction increase while its earlier and cruder emphasis on the development of a repressive apparatus decreased concomitantly. This shift in emphasis was apparent in a number of areas. To begin with, the state began to take responsibility for many of the social functions previously performed by such private groups as the churches and the plantations, including education and health, because without these the spread of commodity production was hampered. Second, the state significantly improved many of the economic functions that it had previously performed, from the postal service to providing the legal framework for joint-stock company operations to the enactment of banking and insurance laws and regulations. Third, in some territories the state took over responsibility for infrastructural works—roads, drainage, irrigation, etc.—from the plantations.

The colonial state took over the functions of economic reproduction in order to facilitate, under the guidance and patronage of the Colonial Office, the development of the new imperialist division of labor and the entrenchment of market relations in the process of internal accumulation. To achieve this the local state, still comprised of colonial officials and planters elected on a restrictive franchise and backed by the colonial power, resolutely sought to promote the *political* interests of the local classes that supported this grand design. This, however, was no longer a straightforward matter, and the social struggles that ensued had a major effect in the form and content of the postcolonial state. The conflict between the emerging local class of educated professionals, local commercial interests, and local landlords, on the one hand, and the expatriate and local groups that represented the interests of plantation agriculture on the other was growing. In many colonies property qualifications for the franchise were reduced; in some this led to the "electoral" defeat of the local planter class, thus halting their direct participation in the machinery of government. But this defeat in turn led the colonial authorities to mount two arguments in the planter class's favor, one social and the other racial. For the first, it was argued that if the planter and large commercial interests failed to win elections and control the local state, those who by their very association with the major commercial activities made them best "equipped" to rule were excluded. Second, the losers were white and the winners nonwhite and the colonial authorities, surreptitiously if not openly, supported the commonly held view that "in no colony the white element should be subject to the coloured, whether it be black, brown or yellow."[1] Given the prevalence of this attitude, the only way for the rising petty bourgeois strata to move forward was for it to widen the struggle. In the early phases, they emphasized the effort to widen the franchise, since it was felt that this would strengthen their numbers and thus the weight of their position with the Colonial Office and the local planter class. Nevertheless, their struggle was viewed by the planter class, and for a long time by the Colonial Office itself, as a struggle to overthrow colonial rule and the economic predominance of plantation agriculture in its entirety.

This was not a true reading of the intentions and aspirations of the emerging elites, however, and the reaction of the Colonial Office and local planters showed their lack of understanding of the system they had created and still benefited from. They failed to realize that there were larger social and economic forces that supported their continued dominance, and instead frequently and needlessly pitted themselves against the newly rising social forces. Just as slavery could not exist indefinitely, so too the vast majority of the population could not indefinitely be excluded from the process of government. Eventually, although reluctantly, the Colonial Office abandoned the planters' view—which it had originally championed—and, while a fear of the black masses remained, a more realistic view of the result of broadening the franchise gained the upper hand.

A final development during this period was that the first tentative steps were taken toward the formation of the ideological and cultural "apparatuses" of the state. As access to education grew, the merits of bourgeois political democracy— particularly as idealized in the so-called Westminster model of parliamentary rule—were emphasized. In colonies with "backward populations" the model was interpreted to mean "orderly constitutional advance," which meant that the masses were considered to be incapable of self-rule for the time being. The Colonial Office was therefore to be the "trustee" of the interests of the masses during a long and orderly series of constitutional steps forward. The franchise was to be progressively widened, an increasing number of functions were to be passed from the Colonial Office to the local government, a multiparty political system was to be instituted, orderly changes in government based on honest electoral practices were to be established, and the rule of law and the independence of the judiciary were to be secured. Virtually every prominent local personality subscribed to the approach, with only minor differences in emphasis. Practice, however, was in marked contrast to the ideal. The stark truth was that the decision to allow only limited self-government reflected a deepseated fear of the masses on the part of both the Colonial Office and the planters, so that Britain reserved the right to intervene in support of any Colonial Office policy that was resisted by the local legislature, including the right to "suspend" the constitution if the decision of the (albeit limited) electorate did not adequately reflect metropolitan interests.[2]

4. National Independence and the Colonial State

Colonialism and resistance

As the colonial period came to a close and the nationalist movement's agitation for political independence gained ascendancy, important changes took place in state and political relations in the colonies. While most of these reflected the maturing of tendencies that had developed during the long period of colonial domination, the intensification of the struggle for national independence after World War II was so marked as to warrant separate treatment here. The nationalist confrontation between the colonial authorities and the local population over "independence" led to changes that were greatly to influence the nature of the state in the postcolonial period.

By World War II, colonial political domination and its accompanying colonial state apparatus were no longer necessary for the economic and social domination of the center over the periphery. Center-periphery relations were by now an integral part of the social system of these countries and stemmed directly from the stage of capitalist development in Europe and the forms of accumulation that accompanied this—the emphasis on the export of capital, the establishment of overseas branch plants, the securing of direct or indirect control of foreign resources, the role of foreign markets in investment decisions, and so on. It was now possible for the developed capitalist countries to impose their forms of accumulation on old and new colonies alike; it was no longer a country's political status that was at issue, but the nature and lack of resilience of its less technologically efficient—and even moribund—precapitalist social relations. While colonial political status clearly reduced the ability to be resilient, its absence was not enough to guarantee resistance to capitalist domination. Socioeconomic relations between the center and the periphery, rather than formal colonial status, formed the basis of the center's domination at this time.

The result was that resistance to European colonial domination now had to take an anti-*imperialist* form. Political independence did not—and could not in these circumstances—mean an end to external domination. Furthermore, to be effective resistance had to be worldwide in scope; that is, it had to embrace the entire periphery, since imperialism itself was a world system that embraced both former and new colonies (with the exception of those ex-colonies, such as the United States, Canada, South Africa, Australia, and New Zealand, where the capitalist mode of production had by this time become dominant). In other words, imperialism was a world system that could only be defeated if it was mobilized against on a sufficiently wide scale. And indeed, the nationalist, anti-imperialist movement moved rapidly to embrace all of Africa, Asia, Latin America, and the Caribbean. And while within each society resistance took its own particular form, this did not simply mean that its roots were in one or another aspect (social, national, racial) of a territory, but were located in the functioning of capitalism as a world system and in the conjuncture at which this system had arrived.

For purposes of analysis, we can note three developments that were to leave a legacy on the operation of the global system. First, there had developed in the previous period (the late 1920s and 1930s) a profound crisis of accumulation in the main capitalist centers, which was compounded by the economic dislocation caused by World War I. The combined effect of these produced high levels of unemployment, vastly underutilized factory capacity, a collapse of credit mechanisms, reduced profits and intense national competition for markets, resources, etc. The impact of these developments on international trade and payments was rapidly generalized, with the result being a depression that quickly became worldwide in scope. This great depression dramatically highlighted the extensive interconnections of the capitalist world economy, removing any lingering doubt among the ruling classes about the global consequence of interrupting the process of capital accumulation in any of the major capitalist economies. This experience was taken seriously, and in the post-World War II period international economic regulation, through such institutions as the General Agreement on Trade and Tariffs, The International Bank for Reconstruction and Development, and The International Monetary Fund, and regional economic integration, through such institutions as the European Economic Community, and national economic regulation, based on Keynesian stabilization and anticyclical policies, came to characterize the "normal" responsibilities of the capitalist state in the center countries.

The decline in profitability that underlay crises of accumulation, together with the accompanying decline in the living standards of the masses, led to an intensification of class conflict within the main capitalist centers as capitalists struggled to recompose their capital stock, reduce wage costs, and raise profitability, and as workers fought to protect their living standards by relying heavily on the leverage of their trade union organizations and their "political votes." Indeed, in the 1930s such crises were sufficiently severe to give birth to a new type of capitalist state, the fascist state, such as emerged in Germany and Italy and to a lesser extent Spain and Portugal, and which was only dislodged (in the case of Germany and Italy) by military defeat in World War II. The third important development was the October Revolution and the national consolidation of socialism in the Soviet Union. At the time this seemed to point in the direction of future workers' struggles, even as it heralded the formation of a new social system capable of contesting capitalism on a world scale.

It is from these three developments that the "three great revolutionary streams" of resistance to exploitation and domination in the post-World War II period arose: the nationalist, anti-imperialist movement in the periphery, the capitalist-worker conflict in the main capitalist countries, and the struggle between socialism and capitalism for dominance in the global mode of production. This formulation is an overly schematic view, and ignores important areas of racial, religious, sexual, and cultural struggle, but it does point to the global and national dimensions of the transformations that occurred during this period. For our purposes, the most important development was the breaking of the connection between imperialism and colonialism. As we shall see in Part 2, political independence did not bring an end to exploitation.

The pre-independence colonial state

While the colonial state was ultimately dominated by the colonial power, the rise of nationalist forces led to a struggle for national control. The dominance of the colonial power was constitutionally effected through the office of the governor, whose veto power made it absolutely clear that colonial interests would never be seriously threatened. Demands for constitutional advance were usually expressed as a demand to expand the area of "local self-government," which amounted to a demand to reduce the power of the office of governor over both day-to-day and policy matters. Yet since the "rules of the game" permitted arbitrary and authoritarian reversals of constitutional advance by the Colonial Office, constitutional advance could not become permanent simply by virtue of being constitutional. One of the best-known reversals was the suspension of the constitution of Guyana in 1953, 137 days after the first (and only) Marxist-led government in a Caribbean colonial territory was *elected* to office under a constitution based on universal adult suffrage.

The movement toward universal suffrage, internal self-rule, independence, and so on therefore depended above all on the state of social struggle and the capacity of the nationalist movement to defend its gains. In other words, the constitutional struggle was always connected to deeper social considerations having to do with the nature of the class struggle locally and with the issue of which class wielded political power. This in turn meant that these struggles were necessarily situated in the larger context of the anticolonial and anti-imperialist struggles.

Since this period was one of acute crisis for the colonial system—the link between imperialism and colonialism having been broken—the colonial power saw its primary task as that of encouraging the development of local elites that would be accommodating to colonial interests and also as that of devising state forms through which the essential—if not the old—forms of dependent relations could be secured. More precisely, the independent state, and those who controlled it, had to be structured so that they would operate in ways that would sustain the existing international division of labor and reproduce the world market within the national economy. In order to ensure this, however, it was crucial that state power not pass to the masses and that in any "balancing" of interests between foreign and local capital in the colonies, the former would always remain dominant. While this was the general pattern attempted, the details conformed to the social-political-economic-cultural realities of each territory.

The main dimensions of state policy during this period can thus be summed up as follows:

(1) The colonial authorities accepted the general view that in the colonies the peasants' hunger for land was the root cause of social discontent. The policy for alleviating this situation varied and was adapted to local peculiarities. In the Caribbean a system of land grants was introduced and peasants encouraged to diversify their crops, reducing in a limited way the overspecialization in export staples. Such diversification was premised, however, on the new crops being compatible with the maintenance of the domination of the export crops—and, in the Caribbean, with the continued domination of the plantation system. State intervention was also oriented toward the support of individual "progressive" farmers, so that land grants served to accentuate the tendency toward individual property-holding and class stratification in the rural areas. Even where cooperatives were established by the colonial authorities, these paid only lip service to the idea of self-reliance and were stifled by the colonial state.

(2) Whatever efforts the state made in the direction of diversification—or, for that matter, industrial development—the inherited configuration of resource use was still seen as rational and as constituting the main pillar of the economy. The policy of the colonial state was therefore to strengthen this configuration. The colonial authorities felt that the local state should be "rational" in the exercise of its economic functions,

meaning that it should encourage the production and export of those products in which it had a "comparative advantage" and import the rest of its requirements. In addition, because technology, capital, managerial skills, etc. could only come from abroad, foreign capital had to be welcomed, and an open door policy was scrupulously supported by the state. Since comparative advantage was determined by natural, racial, and cultural endowments, the colonies were condemned to being producers of primary tropical agricultural staples and minerals for processing overseas, while industrialization—except for certain light import-substitution industries which foreign capital could develop in "partnership" with local capital—was considered impossible. To ensure the commercial feasibility of light industry and to attract capital, local states were encouraged to institute a program of income tax holidays, accelerated depreciation allowances, duty-free import of raw materials, and even the construction of factory facilities to be rented out for nominal rates.

(3) This obvious intensification of the economic role of the state was accompanied by the creation of a number of new organs of administration: rudimentary national economic "planning" agencies were established in most colonies, along with agencies regulating the public utilities, a department to provide statistical services, labor and employment exchanges, and so on. The ultimate objective was to use the state to impose some "order" on the process of domestic accumulation and to orient the economy toward "development." In this regard, the interventionist role of the state in development matters was being established, even before political independence.

(4) The state also encouraged the growth of a strata of local entrepreneurs and businesspeople, in the belief that this would lead to expanded employment opportunities, and would cultivate a "spirit of enterprise" in the community and strengthen the hold of capitalist ideology. To facilitate this, systems of credit and technical aid, along with fiscal incentives to small businesses, were established. An effort was also made to secure the formation of local capital markets.

(5) The range of welfare services—including education, health, community development, old-age pensions—was wid-

ened. These also became unambiguously the responsibility of the state, thereby marginalizing the role played by the plantations, churches, and other private groups.

(6) Finally, in order to meet the growing demands of the working class and to defuse intensified agitation, an attempt was made to regularize the status of labor. Legal obstacles to the formation and functioning of trade unions were removed and these, together with the creation of departments of labor, became the principal institutions regulating the new system of industrial relations.

Considerations for a Marxist theory of the state in the periphery

Several important considerations for a general Marxist theory of the state emerge from an examination of this period. To begin with, despite the fact that the roots of the nationalist movement lay in the "three revolutionary streams" identified earlier, and with the exception of those cases in which wars of national liberation succeeded in smashing the colonial state, (i.e., Vietnam), national independence settlements were based on the exclusion of the masses from effective control of the society. The real and continuing strength of colonialism and imperialism, along with the inherent weaknesses of the petty bourgeois leadership that dominated the nationalist movement, made this possible. The petty bourgeoisie, which viewed itself as the group best constituted to develop these societies after independence, was not, however, in favor of a revolutionary transformation of internal class relations that would place the workers and peasants in control.

Second, this exclusion of the masses from real power was neither accidental nor shortsighted, and accorded with the long-term interests of the colonial power; it was this exclusion, therefore, which constituted the principal social basis on which the postcolonial state—and its authoritarian version—was founded.

Third, despite the many limitations of the nationalist movement, it did achieve major advances when compared with the era of naked colonialism. Above all, it contributed to the dismemberment of the system of colonial empire, and to the severing of the link between imperialism and colonies. And it was the breaking of this link that constituted the necessary, although not sufficient, condition for the development of real alternatives to the exploiting colonial state form.

Fourth, out of this period of anticolonial agitation came the first real mass politics, and along with it the fuller development of an array of mass organizations, including political parties and trade unions. As we shall see later, this particular development, and the extent to which it was able to continue, was an important factor in determining the direction of development of the state in the postcolonial period.

Fifth—and this is linked to the preceding point—the real significance of the constitutional struggles of this period was that they were part of mass action aimed at achieving gains in the socioeconomic field. In other words, political and constitutional advance, no matter how much they appeared to dominate the formal political debates of the period, were always linked to struggles in the socioeconomic domain. This does not, however, mean that all of these struggles had as their first objective improving the condition of the working class; frequently they were confined to demands for improving the position of the emerging petty bourgeoisie, which used mass action as the lever against the colonially entrenched ruling classes and the colonial authorities. This manipulation was in fact a vital feature of almost all of the "independence settlements."

Finally, this point can be extended one step further and it can be argued that the constitutional struggles against the colonial state form were inseparably linked to other struggles and that these, which were not won, had to continue into the post-independence period. This would include struggles against the colonial division of labor and its emphasis on primary commodity production, export specialization, and minimal industrial development; against forced trade and financial links with the metropole, designed to reproduce the world market internally (through currency boards, tariff policies, imperial preferences, etc.); against foreign personnel filling crucial executive/management positions in the upper echelons of state and the private sector; and against the limited autonomy of all local economic, political, and social institutions. These aspects of the colonial state, together with those established in earlier periods, form the kernel out of which the postcolonial state developed. They must be kept in mind as we turn to our analysis of the authoritarian state, since it is out of this historical situation that the authoritarian state developed.

Part 2
National Independence
and the Rise of the
Authoritarian State

5. Class Structure and the State in the Periphery

In Part 1 we saw that in order to unravel the complexities of the colonial state it was first necessary to locate it in the socioeconomic structure of the colony and the relations between colonizer and colonized. This makes an objective determination of this form of state possible and is methodologically the same as making a historical materialist analysis of the state in other class-structured social systems. In my presentation I was at pains to point out that although the colonial state was class-determined, it was never simply the creation of the colonial-imperial power, the local ruling classes, or both. It is important to be aware of this since in some postcolonial situations the "exceptional" rise of a charismatic leader has often blurred both the continuities and the disjunctures in the passage from colonial to postcolonial state structure. My first task in this part of the study is therefore to demonstrate the structural determination of the postcolonial state in the postcolonial society. In order to do this, I will briefly present the key features of the socioeconomic structure of these societies. Before doing that, however, I want to present some considerations arising from the impact of national independence per se on the state structure of these societies, because they have a direct bearing on the socioeconomic structures.

National independence and the nation-state

Despite the leading role played by the workers and peasants in the anticolonial and national liberation struggles in the colonies, the post-World War II independence "settlements" were generally marked by a transfer of state power from the colonial authority to that section of the petty bourgeoisie that it most favored. As we noted above, this petty bourgeoisie had been able, because of the colonial context, to "assume" the leadership of these struggles. Exceptions were few and confined to societies where resistance to independence was so violent that it led to a general war of national liberation, resulting in the destruction of the effective presence of the colonial-imperial power and its client state apparatus. In no other circumstances did these settlements represent an effective seizure of power by the masses—let alone the destruction of the colonial state and the transformation of its colonially structured power relations. And in fact the section of the petty bourgeoisie that shared in these settlements found them very much to its liking, since, like the colonial power before it, it was in the petty bourgeoisie's objective interest to use the state machinery to preserve existing relations of alienation and domination in tact.

It would be an analytical error, however, to assume that because the colonial state machinery was not "smashed," and the masses were effectively excluded from this transfer of power, that these forms of "political independence" had no real significance. In contrast to the popular "radical" view, therefore, this transition was not of a purely formal type, although certain formalities attended it—flag and national anthem, new constitution, membership in the United Nations, and so on. Such an analysis ignores the significant expansion of state functions and the modifications of methods of rule that of necessity followed independence, and leads to a serious misunderstanding of the qualitative leap involved in the transition from colonial to postcolonial state structure. The most important aspects of this expansion were as follows:

(1) *A diversification of foreign relations and foreign trade.* This can be seen in the immediate membership in the United Nations and its related organizations (UNCTAD, IMF/World Bank); in efforts to develop economic links with China, the Soviet Union, and the East European socialist countries; in efforts to form, or join, regional economic groupings and other Third World movements (the nonaligned movement; the "new international economic order"); and in the establishment of diplomatic relations with a broad range of countries. While the

pursuit of these policies varied from country to country, its thrust has generally been to strengthen national sovereignty by creating a national space in the international system, a necessary task for any country in the existing world of nation-states. The movement in this direction has not of course always been linear. Sometimes at the time of independence (and often as a condition of that independence), pacts and agreements (military and otherwise) have been entered into with the former colonial power or with the United States, which run counter to the general aims of the new state and constrain the effective exercise of national sovereignty. Similarly, membership of certain international organizations (i.e., the IMF or the World Bank) has in some cases become a constraint on the exercise of national sovereignty because of the structural deformation of the new nation's economy, fluctuations in global, regional, and national rates of capital accumulation, and the conditions attached to loans obtained from these institutions that were made necessary by these very difficulties. Despite all this, however, an important dimension of the postcolonial state is the move toward diversification and patterns of international relations more in keeping with the politically independent status.

(2) *The expansion of the state into the rural economy.* Principally under the guise of efforts at continued agricultural diversification and self-sufficiency in food production, and in keeping also with the pursuit of the national interest, this expansion in rural society (from whence the bulk of the population generally derives) has been one of the most significant postcolonial developments. However this is done—through rural development projects, the establishment of marketing boards, the provision of electricity and piped water—and regardless of the real objective, the rapid expansion of the state into the rural sector has added a new dimension to the state and its relation to "civil" society.

(3) *The creation of an industrial sector.* In this area the efforts have been aimed primarily at setting in train and/or consolidating the colonially initiated industrialization process, which was based on import substitution. While the familiar problems of dependence on foreign capital, technology, and markets constrain such state expansion, the continued promo-

tion of import-substituting industrialization—even though it is in alliance with foreign capital and is based on the establishment of branch plants by transnational enterprises—has led, in all the societies under consideration, to some degree of diversification of the national economy, and in the process to the development of classes and/or strata that thrive on this dependent industrialization. In the process, the state has added a significant new dimension to its structure.

(4) *The creation of certain other national institutions.* Under this rubric are a variety of state activities that were prompted by the backwardness of the economic structures of these societies including national institutions concerned with such problems as the regulation of markets and the financial system, the direction and control of investments (domestic and foreign), the regulation of wages and prices, the provision of social services, the regulation of foreign trade, and so on. The establishment of these national institutions was a significant development in all postcolonial states, and their overall aim (when combined with the efforts at diversification mentioned in (2) and (3)) was to: (a) minimize the social cost and social disorganization that are inherent when foreign investment is the "engine of growth"; (b) correct the distorted colonial structures of production, which become an inadequate basis for the development of indigenous capital, whether private or state; (c) enhance the position of local capital vis-à-vis foreign capital, particularly in terms of control over resources, technology, marketing, and skills; and (d) enhance state control over the society as a whole by controlling the use and disposition of the means of production and the workforce.

(5) *The expansion of state property.* All the above listed features combine to make these recent postcolonial states strongly "interventionist" in their pursuit of development. While this aim has (rightly) been criticized for being too crudely equated with enhancing the wealth and status of the ruling petty bourgeoisie, and of being in other ways oriented in favor of a small part of the population, it has nevertheless been accompanied by an effort to "localize" ownership of the means of production and therefore to take over certain decision-making powers. This effort has followed three main paths: management

substitution, local share issues and capital market development, and—promoted as the most radical of all— nationalization.¹ This has meant that despite the various ideological stances taken by ruling regimes in the periphery, there has been in every case a dramatic expansion in state control over property (as well as in the state regulation of the economy mentioned in (4)). This has been true in the recently independent states as well as in the older states of Latin America, and is even evident in those countries where there has recently been a trend toward "denationalization" (i.e., Brazil).

In fact, in some countries nationalized property has become the major economic foundation of the state. The economic impact of this is multiplied by state regulation of the licensing of trade and production, tax expenditure policies, and credit and scarce foreign exchange, along with state intervention in the training of the labor force. All these integrate the state into the structure of production, and demonstrate the complexity and extent of the role of the state in these societies. In addition, the expansion of state property has been accompanied by the militarization, bureaucratization, and ideologization of state activities, which has important consequences for class structure, the level of class consciousness, and the nature of class action in these societies. All of these will be discussed in detail later, but here the point should be made that—contrary to certain "left" assertions—the comparison of state property and state control is in no way correlated with the extent of the influence of the masses in the society; on the contrary, such control frequently constitutes the crucial vehicle for arbitrary and repressive acts *against* the masses and their organizations.

Having made these points, we can go on to make a few further observations. One is that the expansion of the role of the state in these economies is not a "voluntary" development, but is structurally and organically linked to the requirements of internal accumulation in these countries. In other words, these states do not expand their role in the national economy for ideological and/or propagandistic reasons, or because of the wishes of a particular leader, but because *all* regimes in the periphery are impelled to do so by the structural necessities of their internal social situations and the historically formed links between their economies and those of the center. That is why, irrespective of their differences, the state in Tanzania and Kenya, or Jamaica and Grenada, is equally expansionist and interventionist.

A second observation is that despite the continued domination of foreign capital after independence, and the growth of what have been called "neocolonial" relations, there is an anti-imperialist thrust to the operations of almost all of the states in the periphery, and particularly the recent postcolonial ones. This can be seen in the official support given to demands for a new international economic order or for "nonalignment in international relations." And whatever local variations may exist in interpreting these objectives, or in the methods used to pursue them, these demands always constitute an effort to redefine the existing international division of labor and geographical distribution of power, which are at present based on the premise of hegemonic imperialist relations. In some states (i.e., Mozambique, Tanzania), this anti-imperialist thrust is tied to a declared "socialist" objective, but it has also (as in Jamaica and Malaysia) been tied to the development of an indigenous capitalist class that it is hoped will resist foreign domination and promote internal growth and hence national interests. This has in turn led these states to take contradictory positions at different times on international issues.[2]

A third observation is that the postcolonial state is almost universally a more politically "legitimate" state than was the colonial state. This is the result of the expansion of the state into the economic, social, and ideological domains described above, but it is also directly linked to the growth of mass politics, one of the main elements of the national liberation movement. While it is true that in many of these societies the mass politics of the nationalist movement is rapidly transformed into state control of popular/mass organizations, it is also true that in the first phase of the transfer of power to the local state the level of mass politics is sufficiently striking as to constitute a key feature of political relations. The rapidity with which this process of mass mobilization and politicization is terminated after independence, and the degree of legitimation obtained by the state, varies, but as a rule it is during the *immediate* postcolonial period that these states achieve their greatest legitimacy. This, combined with the developments noted previously, strengthens the postcolonial state in comparison with its colonial predecessor.

My analysis of this period is in direct opposition to the analysis of many other scholars. Carl Stone, for instance, states:

> With the transfer of state control from imperial to local interests in the period following World War II, the power of the state diminished in both the domestic and international domains which lacked connection with metropolitan economic and military strength. Secondly, whereas in the colonial period state power was integrally connected with the hegemony or effective control of locally relevant economic forces by the imperial power, in the postcolonial or neocolonial (stage two) period, the state no longer exercises hegemony in this sense.[3]

Stone's point of view is premised on the simple idea that the colonial state was stronger because it had the colonial power behind it, with the local state as merely its local representative. However, as I pointed out earlier, even in the period of direct colonial rule intervention was not as automatic a possibility as this formulation implies. A certain degree of autonomy was always accorded to the local state. The colonial power expected that the interests of local ruling groups would in general be in harmony with those of metropolitan capital, but where conflict became so acute as to lead to physical resistance by the local ruling classes, it sometimes led to national independence and secession from the empire. The local state was always, therefore, *potentially* autonomous vis-à-vis the colonial power.

On the other hand, and again contrary to Stone, the threat of a "Communist takeover" or "civil disorder" can still elicit military and economic support from the former colonial power, the United States, or both, even where formal legal agreements to this effect do not exist. Imperialist aggression remains an important feature of the postcolonial situation, as recent events in Chad, the Caribbean, and Central America show. Finally, the local ruling classes continue to maintain close links with international capital, and this permits the continued domination of the working people in postcolonial societies. This, combined with the increased range, influence, and legitimacy of the postcolonial state, suggests that, save for exceptional historical situations (i.e., the territorial disintegration of Zaire in the immediate postindependence period), the postcolonial state is *strengthened* relative to the colonial state.

Social structure and class

The sum total of classes, social strata, and groups, and their system of interconnections, form the social structure of a society. Here I will not attempt a lengthy description of the social structure of the periphery, but only point to those characteristics that are important to the analysis of the state.

(1) The class structure of the periphery is more complex and also generally much weaker—by which I mean that classes are in an early phase of formation and are impeded from further development by economic and other structural features—than in the capitalist center countries. Consider the following illustrations:

The working class. In peripheral societies the classic industrial proletariat is underdeveloped. The working class that exists is often concentrated in four areas—the mineral extractive sector, large-scale plantation-type agricultural enterprises, the emerging import-substitution sector, and the service sector. The first two are traditional colonial sources of wage labor. The third is oriented toward manufacture and/or assembly of consumer goods for the local high-income and urban markets. These enterprises are generally branch plants of transnational corporations and operate under local governments. While the emphasis has been on consumer goods for domestic consumption, production of intermediate goods, capital goods, and manufactured exports is beginning. The service sector occupies a large proportion of the labor force. The enterprises here, however, tend to be small-scale (except for the government sector) and concentrated in the urban areas (except where a tourist sector is highly developed). In addition, a large proportion of the labor force—particularly young people between the ages of 18 and 26—is "structurally unemployed."

Certain features of this configuration of the working class are crucial. One is that the working class is typically distributed among enterprises that are large and small, foreign and local; it is also highly concentrated in urban settlements and in isolated communities. A significant proportion of the female labor force works as lowly paid domestics in individual households and in the recently established "export-processing zones," where imported items such as clothing and electronic products are assembled for re-export back to the center, under the aegis of a transnational corporation. Firms operating in these zones show an overwhelming preference for female employees. This complexity is compounded by the lack of unionization of the wage-labor force, which is seldom more than one-third unionized; even then, the unionized sector is concentrated in large-scale enterprises. The fact that employment is spread among a large number of small establishments has hindered unionization, as well as the development of a sense of class identity, class solidarity, and united class action. The fact that small-scale employment predominates even in the urban areas means that working-class organization is weak even in politically critical areas—i.e., areas that house the seat of government, the administrative headquarters of the political parties and trade unions, and have the largest concentrations of students. There is also considerable geographical mobility, so that workers may live and work in one area (a city, mining town, tourist resort, or large agricultural estate) but maintain a household in a distant area (a rural community). Sometimes the migration is international, and households are split over huge distances. In addition, substantial sections of the working class have some access to private property, from which they supplement their income—i.e., self-operated taxis, small landholdings, small stores, etc. Significant sections have skills that they sell on a part-time, spare-time basis, i.e., female higglers, seamstresses, carpenters, electricians. These links to small property complicate the structure of the working class, its perceptions and behavior.

A significant dimension has been added to the local class structure by the rapid expansion of the lower level salariat that is paid by the state—clerical workers, teachers, nurses, messengers, dispatchers, drivers, and other such service workers. As a result of global economic crises, particularly the long structural depression in economic activity that began in the mid-1970s, this section of the workforce has not only grown, but has tended to develop something of a traditional working-class outlook in its effort to deal with the state as its employer. As a consequence, the more the state becomes directly involved in production and the appropriation of surpluses, the more involved it has become in the industrial areas of working-class struggles.

The propertied classes. A similar complexity is found among the propertied classes. The traditional landed oligarchy, representing "feudalism in the countryside," and the emergent industrial bourgeoisie, representing "capitalist relations in the cities," are not clearly demarcated. Indeed, they may overlap in one person or in one family, creating a complex intertwining of feudal, other precapitalist, and capitalist property relations. Sometimes the landed oligarchy develops out of foreign penetration and settlement, as in the Caribbean, while sometimes it has indigenous roots in the preconquest class structure, as in Africa. The structure of the peasantry as a landholding class is equally complex, because this category includes a wide variety of tenancies, small and medium peasants, "kulaks," any or all of whom may earn a substantial proportion of their income from wage labor on state projects, private haciendas, plantations, and so on, as well as in a number of artisanal and craft-type activities. In addition, the concept of "middle class" is especially vague in these societies because it is a complex category that includes the lower ranks of landowners, professionals, including teachers, middle-level management in state and private enterprises, small-scale commercial operators, shopkeepers, artisans, and traders who work on their own account or with family labor. The vagueness of "middle class" as a category is revealed by the fact that elements usually included in it can also be classified into other groupings; for example, the lower ranks of the landowners can also be classified as richer peasants, while professionals can be included as part of the bourgeoisie. The middle class is sometimes equated with what is called the "intermediate strata," which is a term used to fill the middle ground or gap between the relatively clearly defined peasantry and working class and the major propertied classes (landlords and manufacturing bourgeoisie).

The state and petty bourgeoisie. The most significant post-colonial development, and one that underlines the complexity of the local class structure, is the growth of certain groups and strata associated with the postcolonial expansion of state property.

As noted in the previous section, despite the variety of factors that precipitated the development of these groups, the considerable variation in the social circumstances in which they developed, and the various guises under which this development has been ideologized (i.e., decolonization, socialist construction, or sheer pragmatic necessity), distorted colonial production structures have required all recent postcolonial states to enhance the role of these groups in the economic system. Because the expansion of state property is so common, it appears to be independent of the political status of the class struggle in each territory, or indeed of other national and social considerations. State property, however, is a legal and juridical relation and as such its mere existence is not an accurate reflection of the social relations within the society.

The expansion of state property in peripheral capitalist societies has occurred principally through "nationalization" of foreign property. It is common in some radical—and not so radical—circles to dismiss nationalization as little more than the state-negotiated purchase of foreign assets (at a mutually agreed-upon price), leading to a change in the form of property without any change in its capitalist content. But if we look at a deeper social level, we find that the acquisition of state property in these societies has in fact been an essential element in the process of creating an economic base for the reproduction of the ruling class. As I have argued elsewhere,

> despite the different degrees of importance . . . these various policies attach to the freedom of private ownership of property and the freedom of markets, they are all fundamentally characterized by the deliberate intention of using the state apparatus as a principal instrument of developing a strong class formation, capable of assuming the responsibility of raising the level of de-

velopment of the productive forces. Traditionally, in the context of highly developed class societies, socialist analysis correctly interprets the state apparatus as the *object* of class conquest and the *instrument* of class rule. In the historical situation that prevails in [peripheral] countries, it is more correct to argue that the state has become, as it were, an *instrument of class creation*. This observation highlights the crucial difficulties which are posed for a socialist analysis of the state by the existence in these societies of what is often only a very immature industrial working force, and an underdeveloped local bourgeoisie.[4]

Under these circumstances, what class aspires to be the ruling class and so dramatizes the complexity of class structure? The answer is the *petty bourgeoisie*. Further, its origins lie in colonial conditions, for under the colonial system this was the only local class that, because of its education and propertied status, had any access to political power. This class includes those who are self-employed, as professionals or in the business and public sectors, local business owners, and a sprinkling of kulaks. Indeed, as we saw in Part 1, the struggle to widen the franchise and expand the representative nature of local government was often a struggle to entrench the petty bourgeoisie within the local state structure. This was only to be expected, since the illiteracy and poverty of the masses (generated by colonization itself) meant their political exclusion, just as the education of the petty bourgeoisie led to its progressive inclusion in the state structure.

In the postcolonial situation, control of state power was the basis through which the petty bourgeoisie sought to confirm its social position as a ruling class, albeit in the larger context of its relationship to imperialism and its superordination to the (often expatriate or overseas) ruling class. In the process of consolidating itself as a ruling class, members of the petty bourgeoisie took on political roles and managerial positions in state enterprises.

The emergence of this sector of the petty bourgeoisie constitutes *the* most important postcolonial development in the class structure of the peripheral capitalist societies. It has been variously described as the "state petty bourgeoisie," the "state bourgeoisie," or the "bureaucratic bourgeoisie." Whichever term is used, its essential features are its control of state property, its "nonantagonistic" relationship to the capitalist class in the center countries, and its reinforcement of the reproduction of capitalist relations, both locally and on a world scale.

Some writers have tried to handle the complexity of the petty bourgeoisie by distinguishing a "politico-administrative" element, comprised of heads of government ministries, top civil servants, the top leadership of the party, etc., and an "economic" element, comprised of heads and higher functionaries of public corporations and other state-supervised economic enterprises.[5] This is not a particularly useful formulation, however, because although these elements are identifiable, members of each have strong kinship and other social ties to the other, as well as to elements of the more traditional petty bourgeoisie, including the military (which has expanded rapidly in all postcolonial societies).

Issa Shivji, in *Class Struggle in Tanzania*, points out that the "bureaucratic bourgeoisie" is neither a bureaucracy nor a bourgeoisie in the classic sense of these terms, since it is clearly a product of, and remains structured into the system of, peripheral capitalism. Shivji also points to certain ideological traits of this sector, three of which are of particular significance here because they underline the complexity, and weakness, of the class structures of peripheral capitalism. First, this sector tends to develop a "nationalistic" outlook, derived from its management of the state in a world of highly competitive nation-states. Second, it frequently seeks to conflate its interests with those of the nation as a whole, thereby reinforcing certain class aspects of its nationalist outlook. Finally, in certain circumstances it reveals a "social-democratic" tendency—that is, a tendency to be anticapitalist without challenging the larger framework of capitalist-labor and imperialist relations, to tone down class antagonisms in its propaganda, and to promote a mixed economy and a certain type of welfarism. While I differ with Shivji over the interpretation of this third feature—a point that will be elaborated upon later—it is nevertheless true that the impact of these traits on the class consciousness of this sector of the petty bourgeoisie is significant indeed.

A fundamental result of the development of state property

and of the sector of the petty bourgeoisie associated with it is the *reversal of the classic relation of economic power to political power* in the development of capitalism in the periphery. In the developed capitalist countries the bourgeoisie won political power after it consolidated its economic power. Thus in the United Kingdom the landed gentry prevailed politically long after the economic ascendancy of the manufacturing bourgeoisie. In the periphery, on the other hand, economic power is consolidated after political power and the state machinery are seized. This development suggests the concept of a "state for itself"—that is, a situation in which the people occupying positions of power in the state use it to promote the economic interests of their group (comprised of family, friends, and political buddies). State power is used to form the nucleus of an indigenous bourgeoisie. In the absence of bourgeois-democratic constitutional restraints, this can lead to the institutionalization of all forms of corruption. This is the key to the rise of corruption in these countries and to the role it has played in enlarging the property held by this class and consolidating its economic base.

It should be pointed out that this expansion of state property in the periphery has seldom been opposed by local private capital, since it is usually directed against the dominance of foreign capital (via nationalization) and not against capital as such. This is not to suggest that disputes have not taken place between local private capital and the state—over the extent of internal regulation of the economy, over foreign exchange policies, and over the desirability of pursuing IMF-type "stabilization" programs. Such disputes occur particularly when there are interruptions and crises in the process of capital accumulation, nationally and internationally. On the whole, however, private capital has benefited from the expansion of the state, and more often than not maintains close links with the state petty bourgeoisie. Indeed, members of the business class frequently move into the state sector when the state needs employees with "entrepreneurial" and "managerial" skills to run the nationalized enterprises.

(2) A second characteristic of class structure in the periphery is that it is more fluid—not only in the movement of individuals between one class and another, but in the changing nature

of the classes themselves and their relative size. A good example of this is the rapid development of new urban-based groupings—i.e., higglers, unemployed youth, etc.—as migration from the countryside to the cities continues. The development of both bourgeoisie and proletariat in the cities, particularly in Africa and Asia, coexists with older forms of social relations— i.e., ethnic groupings—which act as mediating elements in the relations among the new urban classes. The mediation process in turn adds to the fluidity of class relations and at the same time makes them even more complex. Furthermore, the rapid growth of the urban centers is in part the result of the growth of two areas of economic activity, import-substitution industry and small businesses and trading establishments. The growth of the former constrains the growth of the latter, which are ruined by the introduction of machine production into import-substitution industries. This also adds to the fluidity of the class structure.

(3) The economies of the periphery can be described as "multistructured" in that they combine numerous different forms of production and types of economic relations: branch plants of transnational enterprises, state property, peasant subsistence holdings, share-cropping, wage labor, individual/ family traders, artisans, commercial houses, local manufacturing enterprises, and so on. Each in its own way affects national production, accumulation, foreign exchange earnings, and employment, so that monopolistic industrial and commercial corporations are not clearly dominant. Nevertheless, there remains a pattern of specialized production of one or two commodities for sale in the world market, and a heavy reliance on foreign skills, technology, and financing, despite the fact that even this specialized production embraces many different forms of enterprise.

The predominant role of production for the world market leads to a particular type of capitalist relations. In the case of classic European, American, and Japanese capitalism, production was initially impelled by the requirements of the internal market, and internal resources were developed to satisfy that market. The world market then developed as an extension of the domestic market, thereby ensuring that the predominant economic relations were "interiorized." In the typical peripheral capitalist society, however, this interiorization has not occurred. They remain dominated by the impact of colonial expansion and the resulting integration into the world division of labor. Thus, as pointed out earlier, we repeatedly find a dynamic of production-consumption in which domestic resources are used to produce goods for export and internal market requirements are satisfied through imports.

(4) A significant element of the dominant classes in the periphery is foreign, either resident or not. This underlines the fact that the bourgeoisie alone has been able to organize itself as a class at the global level. Further, although there is a foreign sector in the ruling class structure of these societies, it is not a "legitimate" part of the nation-state insofar as neither its members (nor their resident representatives) are citizens. As a result, this sector of the ruling class must find mechanisms to ensure its continued influence. The existence of this sector of the ruling class further complicates social relations and has an important effect on the structure of the state.

(5) In these societies the interaction of class-based and non-property-based social relations is much more important than in the capitalist center countries, where class structures are more clearly defined. Thus in the periphery, ethnic, sex, religion, language, caste, rural/urban divisions, etc. interact with class and make the social structure even more difficult to analyze. This type of interaction has led some social scientists to go so far as to argue that there are no classes in Africa, and led others to argue that, on the contrary, there are *only* class relations. But the coexistence, and interaction, of nonproperty and class relations is the product of the particular stage of development of these societies, and until class structures, class consciousness, and class outlook become more defined, any attempt to understand the social structure of these societies must take the nature and character of this interplay into account.

Conclusion

In concluding this discussion of the social structure of the periphery, let me make a number of observations that have direct relevance to the study of the state. The first of these is that colonialism and external capitalist domination of the social structures of the periphery (particularly the class structure and the economic structure) are crucial factors to be taken into account when attempting to determine the laws of motion of these societies. This point was implicit in earlier statements—that it was the specific nature of colonial domination that facilitated the development of petty bourgeois control of state power, that the independence "settlements" were predicated on the exclusion of the masses from political power, and so on—but it must constantly be kept in mind, since otherwise there can be no real understanding of the dynamic of recent postcolonial states.

A second observation is that in the periphery, where both the traditional classes of the capitalist social formation (workers and capitalists) are underdeveloped, and where both of these classes are small in numbers and qualitatively weak, there is no clearly hegemonic ruling class. Further, the proletariat, while the weaker of the two, has been in existence longer and so demonstrates the existence of the original contradiction between the local working class and foreign capital (even though both the local bourgeoisie and the proletariat developed under the domination of expatriate capital). This phenomenon is associated with peripheral capitalist societies.

A third observation is that the social and cultural conditions under which the working class develops in the periphery frequently produce deep divisions within it. This fracturing of the working class—whether along sexual, ethnic, cultural, or religious lines—has led to racial, religious, and other aspects of a "caste" outlook playing important roles in the formation of class consciousness. This has frequently made it difficult to delineate class lines. Thus while it may be possible to predict, on the basis of past experience, that class consciousness will develop as capitalist relations deepen, at the moment the situation in these societies is too complicated for easy prediction.

A fourth observation is that although the petty bourgeoisie that presently controls state power is not a homogeneous group but includes several fractions—professional, political administrative, state-economic, and private—and although fractional conflict exists, nevertheless in the absence of an entrenched ruling class its self-interest leads it to develop closer relations with national private capital, and the state takes on the characteristic referred to earlier as being a "state for itself."

It is out of this complex situation that a fifth important observation arises, which is that despite the complexity and fluidity of the class structure, the precapitalist influences on class outlook, etc., class struggle nevertheless continues no less sharply than before. Indeed, as we shall see in the following chapters, the development of state property and the consequent role the state has come to play as a major employer of wage labor has enhanced class struggle. The reason is that whereas in developed capitalist societies, where private capital is dominant, the link between worker-capital conflicts and state power is not easily perceived by the general population, where there is a state sector, an underdeveloped economy, and a major on-going structural crisis of world capitalism, the state's employees are able to see the link between the state and the dominant economic interests in the periphery more clearly.

In conclusion, it is worth reiterating a point made earlier: just as it is important to understand the role of colonial domination in the development of the social structure of the periphery, so too it is important to understand the continued influence of international capitalism on this social structure, despite the formal ending of the colonial relationship. In other words, while "postcolonial" is certainly more than a formal description of political status, it does not mean that these societies have been removed from the path of peripheral capitalist development.

6. State Power and Class Power: Autonomization in the Periphery

Before delineating the characteristics of the authoritarian state itself there is one further task to attend to. This is to examine the ability of such a state to operate in an "autonomous" manner in relation to its social base.

In the next two chapters, therefore, I will show how the growth of the authoritarian state is associated with the dominance of the executive branch of the state over all others, and sometimes with the dominance of the political head of this executive branch over all other state institutions. This development often makes it appear that the state functions "autonomously." The ability of states to function in this relatively independent manner is common to *all* state forms, and has been the source of a considerable literature, particularly within the last fifteen years. Here we will examine the basis of this autonomy, its origins, and the features peculiar to peripheral societies that foster its growth.

The relative autonomy of the state

Though Marxist theory places principal emphasis on the class nature of the state, Marx and Engels learned from their studies of Bonapartism, the seventeenth- and eighteenth-century absolute monarchies, Bismarck, Russian tzarism, and Oriental despotism that in a class society, the state in pursuit of its conception of the national interest can function in a relatively "autonomous" or independent manner vis-à-vis the "economically dominant class" and also vis-à-vis all other classes—indeed, vis-à-vis "civil society" itself. This suggests that in class societies the political sphere can, in certain circumstances, exercise a *relatively* independent role in the determination of social change, even though this role is never taken on isolated from the material basis of society or the particular historical context in which it occurs.

Some of the issues in Part 1 are important in understanding the development of this capacity for state autonomy. We saw there that while the colonial state was, in the last instance, sanctioned by the colonial power, it did not evolve independent of the needs of the local society or of its internal class relations. In the Caribbean, for instance, many of the authority functions assumed by the state were organized and administered through the plantations. The institutional transformation from plantation as organizing authority to a local state form was in response to the consolidation of the power of colonial and planter interests; but although the state was a class institution in that it served the interests of the ruling colonial-planter classes in the crudest of ways, there was never an *identity* of state power and class power. Many of the conflicts between the local state and the colonial power, or between different sections of the dominant classes, led to state actions that did not meet the demands of the ruling classes as a whole, or even of the dominant sections of them. In addition, the power of the ruling colonial-planter classes was derived from their overwhelming control of the plantation production structures and their position within the system of colonial administration and domination. It was from their monopoly of ownership and control of the plantations that these classes derived their power to appropriate the product of the direct producers. Therefore, while control of the state certainly served to consolidate their dominant position in the society, the real source of class power flowed from the position which these classes held in the system of commodity production—this being the *material foundation* on which a class develops and from which it proceeds to exercise its domination. There was therefore a clear *nonequivalence* of state power and the power of the ruling classes, a nonequivalence that also points to the potential separation between the exercise of state power and the interests of the ruling classes.

There are, in addition, other vital disjunctures that must be borne in mind when studying the state and political relations in a class society. One derives from the consideration that the highest form of class struggle is political struggle. Historically, as capitalism has developed, political struggle has frequently been made manifest in the organization of political parties more or less along class lines—parties that focus on the struggle to control the government and the state machinery. Political parties, however, differ from the classes they claim to represent. They never embrace the whole of a class; at most they represent the institutionalization of its more conscious, active representatives. Because of this, a second disjuncture is revealed: the lack of identity between political and class relations.

There is a third important disjuncture. This stems from the likelihood, richly supported by historical evidence, that the leadership—or worse, the "leader"—of a political party may become the substitute for the party, thereby creating an even greater separation between political and class relations.

Taken together, these three disjunctures create a situation in which it is difficult for those who control the state machinery to determine the national interest—or even the interest of the dominant economic groups. It is thus possible for those who control the state machinery to pursue a course that is, within limits, independent of the class basis of the state. Taken together, therefore, these disjunctures provide one source of state autonomy.

The dominant role given the ruling class in the analysis of the state should not obscure the fact that no ruling class is entirely homogeneous. Two features of developed commodity production are its competitive nature and its persistent elevation of private interests over social well-being. For these reasons alone, it is inevitable that in any particular situation the dominant economic interests will be fractionalized—that is, divided into a number of individual, particular, and sectional interests, in addition to the interests of the "class as a whole." The state has emerged as the institution best suited to mediate among the ruling-class fractions, but to perform this role effectively it needs a certain amount of social space—that is, it needs a certain degree of autonomy or independence in relation to the ruling class, while still serving it. This constitutes a second source of state autonomy.

Neither analytically nor in actual practice is it possible to reduce the state to a simple instrument of the ruling class, performing and responding to each and every one of its demands. This is true even where the link between those who run the state and those who make up the economically dominant class are strong and explicit, as they were during the heyday of planter-class hegemony in colonial slave society. However, if the link between the political elite and the ruling class is less strong, this does not necessarily mean that the scope for relative state autonomy widens. The reason is that the real basis of state autonomy lies in the competitive pursuit of private commodity production, and the fractionalization of ruling-class interests that this engenders, rather than in whether or not the economically dominant class rules in the political domain.

In peripheral capitalist societies, with their underdeveloped class structures and underdeveloped and heterogenous production structures, it is not possible for any one indigenous class to be *the* economically dominant class—although, as pointed out earlier, the state is frequently used as an instrument to promote the *formation* of such a class. Even given the highly instrumental character of the state, it cannot be reduced to a simple tool of those who control it. Its relation to the class-in-formation is always complex, particularly since the material basis for the expansion of the state is the *restricted* scope of indigenous private capital accumulation (a restriction that is the result of the way these societies have been integrated into the world market and the consequent distorted production structures, narrow base of economic activity, and heterogeneity in levels of production). To serve the overall interests of the ruling class in these circumstances, the state must promote the growth of commodity relations, yet it is constrained from doing so by the dominant structures of these social formations and the interests that cluster around them. Consequently, although privatized production and commodity relations may not be as highly developed in the periphery as in the capitalist center countries, the particularization of interests of the dominant classes remains a principal feature of recent postcolonial societies.

The points made here in connection with this second source of state autonomy are important to an evaluation of Hamza Alavi's influential analysis of the postcolonial state.[1] Alavi argues that it is impossible to speak of a "hegemonic bourgeoisie constituted by varying fractions" because, compared to developed capitalist formations, there is in the periphery a much greater structural heterogeneity of the ruling classes. In Pakistan and Bangladesh—the cases he is analyzing—Alavi proposes that there were three major propertied classes: a landowning (precapitalist) bourgeoisie, an indigenous industrial bourgeoisie, and the ubiquitous metropolitan bourgeoisie of the ex-colonies. Each of these has its own separate economic base and distinctly separate mode of insertion into the system of production. In Pakistan and Bangladesh, the state played a mediating and conciliatory role among the three propertied classes, which constitutes the basis for its relative independence of them. According to Alavi, this differs from the situation in the more developed capitalist formations, where there is a clearly formed hegemonic bourgeoisie and where the fractions that exist are fractions of a single ruling class. In postcolonial formations, no such hegemonic bourgeoisie exists.

Much of the major work on postcolonial states emerged out of the debate that followed the publication of Alavi's paper. First, Girling challenged the assertion that there were three classes in the postcolonial societies Alavi was discussing, arguing that this masked the complex interactions and interpenetrations of the various fractions of the "dominant power bloc" within peripheral capitalist societies and pointing to the interlocking nature of the three supposedly separate ruling classes.[2] Despite the fact that Girling was probably correct in arguing that Alavi misrepresented the nature of the ruling class in Pakistan and Bangladesh, what is significant about Alavi's position from our point of view is his failure to appreciate that ruling-class interests in commodity-producing societies *will always* be fractionalized. This is basic to the Marxian analysis of capitalism, and is true even where there is a hegemonic ruling class. Thus to assert, as Alavi does, that the basis of the relative independence of the state in peripheral capitalist societies differs from that of advanced capitalist societies is to understand the Marxist argument that there are fractions of capital in *all* commodity-producing societies.

It should be pointed out, however, that when Marx argued that in certain circumstances the state in capitalist societies operates relatively independently of the specific interests of the various fractions of the dominant class, this did not mean that at these times the state would no longer serve the ruling class's long-term class objective of securing the reproduction of its hegemony and dominance. My argument is that in peripheral capitalist societies this long-term objective is exercised in relation to the interests and power of one or another fraction of the dominant class.

Alavi's analysis does not end here, however. He goes on to claim that the state in postcolonial societies is "overdeveloped," and that this constitutes another basis for its relative independence. He argues that during colonial rule a state is imposed which is capable of suppressing all the indigenous classes. Such a state has its real basis in the social relations of production in the metropole. Therefore:

> It might be said that the "superstructure" in the colony is therefore "overdeveloped" in relation to the "structure" in the colony, for its basis lies in the metropolitan structure itself, from which it is later separated at the time of independence. The colonial state is therefore equipped with a powerful bureaucratic-military apparatus and mechanisms of government which enable it through its routine operations to subordinate the native social classes. The post-colonial society inherits that overdeveloped apparatus of state and its institutionalized practices through which the operations of the indigenous social classes are regulated and controlled.[3]

Such a feature strengthens the base-superstructure disjuncture and is a further factor in favor of state autonomy.

This thesis of the "overdeveloped" postcolonial state has been critiqued elsewhere.[4] As Colin Leys, for instance, points out in relation to East Africa, "Why should this [situation] call for a particularly strong state if there are no strong social classes to defend their interests in the old social formations?"[5] To which we might add: How do we explain the states of Latin America, which have been independent for over a century and

a half and yet in other respects fall within the category of peripheral capitalist formations? If these states are as "overdeveloped" as Alavi claims, how do we explain major aspects
of their expansion (referred to in earlier chapters), which took
place after independence? The truth is, as others have pointed
out, the concept of "overdeveloped" raises more questions than
it answers. "Overdeveloped" in relation to what? As
W. Ziemann and M. Lazendörfer ask, does it mean that

> the state wields a "strength" greater than is necessary to secure
> the social reproduction? Or does it assume that, in proportion to
> the structure, the superstructure is not too top heavy, but never-
> theless very large? But—very large in relation to what? What is
> the "normal" relation? Obviously the questions are meaningless.
> For so long as a state is fitted for its main function, to secure the
> societal reproduction, the extent of its influence on society is
> neither too great nor too small, but adequate.[6]

John Saul has modified and adapted Alavi's general argument by adding the fact that the postcolonial state takes on the
ideological function with great vigor.[7] He claims that this, combined with the points made by Alavi, means that the postcolonial state acquires a high degree of "centrality" in the social
system, and that this explains its relative autonomy. In other
words, autonomy is rooted in the *central* role the state plays in
peripheral capitalist societies. Again, it is difficult to understand what is so special about this centrality. In all commodity-
producing societies—indeed, in all class societies—the state
plays a central role in social reproduction. To understand how
that role is effected requires an analysis of concrete conditions;
a priori generalization is not enough.

Alavi and Saul have been discussed at some length because
of the important place their work holds in the literature on
postcolonial states. Yet although they have been arguing for a
special nature to state autonomy in peripheral capitalist formations, their formulations in fact go no further than the accepted
Marxian formulation: that essential to the nature of capital is its
fractionalization and division into diverse private interests. In
societies where the capital relation is dominant, the ruling
class or classes will *always* be made up of various fractions. In

this sense, therefore, their arguments add nothing new to the second aspect of state autonomy that is being considered here. The relationship of the ruling class to the state (even where the ruling class is a clearly defined and homogenous group, with substantial ties among its members) is *always* complex, for the ties that bind a ruling class together come into conflict with the fact that society is founded on the private appropriation of what is produced. Indeed, it is recognition of this that permits us to argue for the autonomy of the state in relation not only to the ruling class but to all classes, and to the whole of "civil society" itself.

A third source of state autonomy, one which many consider to be primary, derives from the fact that the separation of state and society has, historically, led to the formation and growth of bureaucracy. The state, because it represents the institutionalization of authority, promotes the rapid growth of bureaucracy within it. One aspect of this is the dominance of the executive within the state structure. As this development has proceeded, the executive has come to display a high degree of autonomy within the state structure with respect to the other organs of the state.

Several factors have given rise to the faster growth of the executive (and its bureaucracy), including the need for continuity in the exercise of authority functions, the growing complexity of these functions, the need to process information in relation to them, and the hierarchic and exploitative nature of commodity-producing societies. The pressures these generate are so strong that the executive and its bureaucracy become the principal agency that pushes toward autonomy for the state as a whole. Indeed, the role of the executive in this process plays a major role in Marx's political commentaries. For instance, in the discussion of Bonapartism, Marx points out that where the executive is strong in relation to other institutions—whether of the ruling or subordinate classes (i.e., trade unions, parliaments, etc.)—the capacity for the independent exercise of executive power is greatly enhanced. Following on this, we can argue that the transitional circumstances in which bureaucracies gain ascendancy, in both the developed and peripheral capitalist formations, make this the dominant feature of state autonomy.

In recent postcolonial societies the growth of the executive branch of the state relative to other branches is often reinforced by constitutional provisions. There are even cases where one person—head of state, head of the executive—is constitutionally given the power to appoint every important state official, is constitutionally made head of the security services, and is constitutionally given the office of leader of the ruling party. In Guyana this equation of person and authority is further reinforced by two political circumstances: an electoral system based on proportional representation (with the "leader" of the winning party free to choose the members of parliament from a list submitted at the time of elections), and the rigging of every election since independence.[8] This is an extreme, but by no means uncommon, event.

A fourth source of state autonomy in capitalist societies lies in what Hal Draper has referred to as the "political inaptitude" of the capitalist class: "Of all the ruling classes known to history, the membership of the capitalist class is least well adapted, and tends to be most averse, to taking direct charge of the operation of the state apparatus. The key word is: direct."[9] Needless to say, this inaptitude stems not from natural but from social causes. Draper goes on to point out that capitalism enjoys the

> deepest separation between its economic and political institutions, . . . its mode of exploitation depends characteristically on the processes of the market, not on politics, which is ancillary and supportive . . . in [the capitalist's] own activity *as a capitalist* he is concerned with nonpolitical preoccupations . . . he wants to make money, not run the government himself.[10]

This is reinforced by the fact that the capitalist class does not develop as what Draper terms a "class of idlers but rather of very busy and hard-working men, working hard at exploiting the productive labor of others,"[11] and because of the direct link between the ruling class and the process of economic production, which stems from its ownership of the major means of production.

Draper further asserts that the private interests and competitive nature of capital require even members of the ruling class to go at "each other's throats," and that "this exuberance of internal hostilities makes it more difficult for any individual capitalist to be trusted as executor for the class as a whole."[12] Out of these social circumstances there develops a breed of "professional" politician who, to perform adequately, cannot simply be a tool or instrument of the ruling class. This would be difficult not only because of the fractionalized and competitive nature of this class, but because the professional politician comes to see that *his own* effectiveness requires a longer view, a more holistic approach to the interests of the ruling class, and therefore struggles to ensure enough autonomy for the state to pursue this vision. The result is that, while the ruling personnel cannot determine the state's class character, the fact that a specialized body of people runs the state promotes a tendency toward the separation of the state from the ruling class.

A fifth source of state autonomy, one whose importance has grown as capitalism has developed, derives from the manner in which the state is inserted into the system of material production and reproduction, and the resulting requirement that it perform an *economic function*.[13] This is more than economic activity as measured by such variables as the state's share of gross national product, employment, national investment, consumption, generation of savings, and so on, but extends to those functions that are essential to the economic process in all societies and cannot adequately be attended to by individuals or groups. These include determining and upholding the legal and statutory forms necessary for commodity exchange; stabilizing the growth of the national product and ironing out fluctuations in accumulation caused by national and international circumstances; protecting the national interests of the economy in the world market; and, more generally, determining the choice of development model pursued by the state. Since class interests, as well as the interests of groups within each class, clash in the economic sphere, the state, as regulator of social conflict, takes on an *economic function* as it tries to resolve these conflicts—for it is in pursuing this function that the state realizes its social objective of ensuring the reproduction of the basic social and class relations of the society. The class character of the state's intervention is therefore evident in the way it is involved in the economic process and the way it tries to resolve economic problems.

At the present stage, the development of the economic function of the state in peripheral capitalist societies is shown in
the growth of state property and the effort to promote an "independent" role for the territory in the world economy, both effected in order to protect the so-called national interest. As we
noted previously, the growth of state property and state intervention in the economy is sometimes rationalized on "socialist" principles, at other times on "capitalist" principles, and
sometimes is said to be "nonideological," the result of "pragmatic" necessity. The reason for these varied presentations is
that the economic function of the state in these formations is
necessarily contradictory. To appreciate this it should be remembered that state intervention in the economy is the product
of complex historical circumstances, in particular of the popular struggle against colonialism. Thus the struggle to create a
national area in the world economy is anti-imperialist (because
it is an assertion of national disagreement with the prevailing
territorial division of labor), even though the principal result of
this state activity is to reproduce world market conditions
within the national economy for the benefit of the local
propertied classes. In other words, one form of capital (foreign)
may be attacked (through nationalization, or calls for fairer
prices for primary products, or criticisms of insufficient aid,
inappropriate technological transfers, etc.) in order to
strengthen another form of capital (indigenous) (i.e., by ignoring domestic monopolies, weakening local trade unions,
undermining peasant producer and marketing associations in
favor of local landlords, etc.). The conclusion which follows
from this contradictory aspect is that in order for the state in
peripheral capitalist societies to pursue its general economic
function it must win relative autonomy from the dominant economic interests. Without this the state would not be able to
intervene in the domestic economic system in order to promote
economic development as it sees fit, to intervene against
foreign capital as it deems necessary, or to promote the "national" interest and protect sovereignty in a highly competitive
international system.

A final source of autonomy derives from the tendency in
peripheral societies where bourgeois norms of constitutionality
are neither well developed nor deeply entrenched for there to

be little of the traditional "separation of powers" among the judicial, executive, and parliamentary organs of the state. Marxists usually react negatively to the doctrine of "separation of powers," claiming that there is an identity of law and state in class societies, with law always subservient to state, and hence to the interests of a particular class. This is incorrect, however. In order to appeal to concepts of justice, fairness, right, and so on, law and its system of administration can never be permitted to operate, or appear to operate, in a crude and obviously class-biased way. Indeed, it is precisely to protect democratic societies that the judiciary, while appointed on the advice of the highest levels of political authority, nevertheless has managed to carve out effective, albeit limited, areas of auton-omy within the state structure (usually based on its power to "interpret" the constitution and the law). Clearly the extent of judicial independence cannot be determined *a priori*, but rests on the course of social development.

This point is all too often ignored by the "left" in its analysis, with disastrous consequences. It is apt, therefore, to recall with Engels that

> in a modern state, law must not only correspond to the general economic condition, and to its expression, but must also be an internally coherent expression which does not, owing to inner contradictions, reduce itself to naught. And in order to achieve this, the faithful reflection of economic conditions suffers in-creasingly. All the more so the more rarely it happens that a code of law is the blunt unmitigated unadulterated expression of the domination of a class—this in itself would offend the "concep-tion of right."[14]

This analysis is consistent with a historical materialist analysis of social development. The superstructure of society (i.e., the totality of the dominant legal, political, artistic, religious, aes-thetic, moral, intellectual, and philosophical ideas of the soci-ety; the institutions through which these are expressed; and the social consciousness of the people) must necessarily have some independence from its base (i.e., the social relations formed by people in the process of their reproduction of the material basis of social life). The relationship of base to superstructure is dia-lectical, not mechanical or rigidly determined. If this is so, the state cannot in any way be seen as either determined by the existing mode of production—even if the state is confined analytically to the superstructure. Once the superstructure is seen as an active force in social development, the basis for the autonomy of the state exists. And if the state is seen as merged with the base, this capacity to be autonomous is even clearer.

Conclusion

All these tendencies toward autonomization do not abolish the class character of the state or transform it into a neutral institution. Contrary to bourgeois political theory—where the state is not the instrument of any class—the state is in fact always preeminently a class institution, even though it can only act for the ruling class under the constraints discussed. And insofar as the state is the central arena for the resolution of political and social conflict, its autonomy may well aid the ruling class in the execution of its class project.

A further point to ponder is Ralph Miliband's observation that the capitalist state has been the organizer of reform *par excellence*. In developed capitalist societies, reforms have been a key means of defusing class antagonisms and resolving social conflicts, and these have been essential to the perpetuation of the hegemony of the ruling class. Miliband argues that the state has had the prime responsibility for the "*organization* of reform" because "what to concede and when to concede—the two being closely related—are matters of some delicacy, which a ruling class, with its eyes fixed on immediate interests and demands, cannot be expected to handle properly."[15] And in order to pursue this reforming function, the state must be able to act independently of the ruling class. This is not a painless process, however, and influential sections of the ruling class do not appreciate the value of these reforms; sometimes their resistance is so strong that an acute political crisis follows, as happened in Europe and the United States in the 1930s.

The resistance to the autonomy of the state, and the accompanying increase in the strength of the executive branch, is not confined to the ruling class. But in capitalist society, since the increase in executive power principally affects the ability of private capital to "direct" the state, resistance has generally been more insistent from this quarter than from others. Indeed, in the political struggle, nonruling classes and groups have championed the expansion of state functions as necessary to protect their interests! This development has led to the growth of social democracy and of the welfare state in developed capitalist countries, while in the periphery it has led to the promotion of "socialism," the protection of national interests against imperialist domination, and the creation of the social "space" necessary for such reforms as the nationalization of foreign property.

It is important when discussing the fractionalization of the ruling class not to argue that the more fractionalized the ruling class, the more independent the state, or—to put it another way—that where no fractions exist, the state cannot be "independent." The point is that whether or not the fractionalization of the ruling class and fragmentation of the society as a whole leads to state autonomy, and the degree of such autonomy, depends on concrete circumstances. Such conditions favor state autonomy, but do not guarantee it. Similarly, the absence of such conditions does not rule out state autonomy for the disjuncture of class power and state power exists *independent* of the internal structure of the ruling class.

In many peripheral capitalist societies the level of internecine struggle is so high that there is a real possibility that the society will disintegrate. Further, because no class is strong enough to impose its solution to the society's problems, a class outlook does not dominate political relations. But even if it did, it must be remembered that class struggle creates the opportunity for revolutionary advance but does not automatically *guarantee* this advance. Every class-divided society is faced with the risk that class struggle may lead to its disintegration and to the "common ruin" of *all* classes. And, if we add to class struggle struggles of a racial, religious, or ethnic character, we can see that the risk of "common ruin" only increases. In such circumstances, the state's claim to be able to preserve the integrity of the society is appealing to all classes, and this in turn favors tendencies that support the autonomy of the state.

In conclusion, it must be emphasized that the autonomy of

the state cannot be viewed onesidedly, that is, as a reflection of the status of contending classes and other social groups. This autonomization is *itself* a necessary factor in ensuring the consolidation of the dominant mode of capital accumulation. In addition, insofar as state investments and state controls are a part of this consolidation and are linked to economic backwardness and the underdevelopment of the major classes, this autonomy *is not necessarily of a short duration.* On the contrary, the "exceptional circumstances" that favor state autonomy in postcolonial societies may last for a long time indeed.

7. The Rise of the Authoritarian State

Class struggle cannot be viewed onesidedly, looking only at the effort of the dominated classes to capture state power and free themselves from the rule of the dominant classes and strata. The reverse must be considered as well: the effort of the ruling classes to perpetuate their domination. This simple truth is often forgotten in the study of peripheral capitalist societies, and particularly in the study of those recent postcolonial countries in which the colonially cultivated ideology has led to illusions about the entrenchment of the practice of "Westminster-style parliamentary democracy" in political life. For these societies it is assumed that, as a result of the "civilizing" mission of colonial rule, political institutions and political behavior are governed by the commitment of the principal actors to a two-party (or multi-party) political system, to a freely elected law-making parliament, to the exercise of executive power by all the authorities of the state (including the government) in such a manner that the officers of the state are held responsible for their actions and so are upholders of the "rule of law," and to an independent judiciary. It is often overlooked by radical theorists, who are understandably preoccupied with the ability of the exploited classes to end their exploitation. This is a mistake, however, for it does not aid the development of a consciousness on the part of these populations about the ruling classes' use of state power along authoritarian lines in an effort to maintain their hegemony. This use of power is only perceived when the ruling classes persist in asserting their "right" to control the state machinery in the face of obviously declining electoral support and political popularity, when they openly resort to the use of the coercive and ideological arms of the state to contain the "opposition," and when they then remove the possibility of any legal or constitutional succession of governments. Even then it is sometimes treated as a temporary aberration. By this time, however, the authoritarian state is already fully formed.

The purpose of this chapter is to discuss in detail the formation, nature, and methods of operation of the authoritarian state. The last three sections amplify on two important subthemes, namely, the relationship of political democracy to the struggle for socialism in the periphery, and the difference between the authoritarian state and the fascist states of Europe and the military dictatorships of Latin America—comparisons that should facilitate our understanding of the authoritarian state itself.

The material basis

Because concepts are only valid in the social sciences to the extent that they are based on a scientific understanding of society, the concept "authoritarian state" cannot, contrary to common practice, be assigned to one form or another of despotic or tyrannical rule, independent of any specific historical or structural context. This would reduce the concept to a general ahistorical structure, without any material content and hence without any scientific validity for the study of society. The authoritarian state as the term is used here is therefore more than a description of a method of rule. It is a social category, and is located in the specific historical and structural context of the reproduction of the material basis of life in peripheral capitalist societies. The preceding chapters have described the historical and structural conditions in which the authoritarian state develops. Here I shall bring together in a schematic but systematic way the essential characteristics of this development in order to elucidate the materialist basis on which this state form develops. In sum, these are as follows:

First, the authoritarian state develops in peripheral capitalist societies characterized by the historically unique combination of underdeveloped productive forces and heterogenous and multistructured modes of economic production. These latter range from branch-plant operations of modern transnational corporations, through state-owned capitalist enterprises, to a variety of precapitalist rural and urban structures of production. Overall, these economies are fractured, distorted, and disarticulated, and have little capacity for self-centered, autonomous accumulation. Irrespective of the form of legal ownership of the means of production, the process of internal accumulation is dependent on the state of accumulation, finance, markets, and technology in the capitalist center countries.

Second, this system of economic reproduction is not recent, but has been occasioned by the colonial manner in which these economies were structurally inserted into the world capitalist system. From the first colonial modes of insertion up to the present-day imperialist linking of the social formations of the center and the periphery, a definite set of links, or chain of capital domination, has regulated this system of economic reproduction.

Third, the combined effect of these two features on the social structure of these societies is twofold: (1) The major classes of the capitalist era (bourgeoisie and proletariat) are underdeveloped. Further, important nonclass social alignments (race, religion, age, ethnicity, sex) play a major role in economic reproduction and in social life in general. (2) The dominant strata, groups, and classes (usually a mixture of petty bourgeoisie, landlords, the military, capitalists associated with import substitution, and so on) are allied with the bourgeoisie of the center because of the ultimate convergence of their interests in favor of the domination of capital. This does not mean that there are no important conflicts between them—there are many, and particularly important are those deriving from national considerations. These help to generate an anti-imperialist posture in the periphery. (Interimperialist rivalry is the form similar conflicts take among the center countries.) What is important here, however, is the extent to which the masses were excluded from political power at the time of the independence "settlements," and have continued to be excluded ever since.

Fourth, this twofold effect results in a leading role to one or more sections of the petty bourgeoisie in the exercise of state power. Thus this class continues in the favored position it has held since the colonial transfer of power to the local state, a continuation that has benefited from the legitimation of state power that was one result of the mass mobilization and mass politics of the anticolonial struggles.

Fifth, the general underdevelopment of capitalist production relations in these societies has restricted the practice of "bourgeois" ideas of legality and equality—classified under the rubric "Westminster-style parliamentary democracy"—among the population at large, particularly since these are founded on the "equality" of all individuals in the marketplace. Because of this, political and legal relations in these societies have not been democratically transformed along bourgeois lines.

Sixth, a rapid growth of state property has taken place, both for states advocating "socialism" and those advocating "capitalism." What is significant here is that while in the capitalist center countries (now, if not in the early periods of their development) state intervention grows out of the cyclical crises that accompany the growth of output, in peripheral societies it is the *absence* of growth, the *scarcity* of capital, frequent *crises* in world commodity markets, and so on that foster state intervention in the system of economic reproduction. In other words, the expansion of state property and the development of state-controlled mechanisms of economic regulation are a *result* of the development orientation of the state.

Seventh, this development of state property expands the potential coercive ability of the state. Every significant expansion of state control over a society's resources and every intervention into "civil" life has the potential of doing this. At the same time, however, this development can—and frequently does—sharpen class contradictions since as state property expands so does the role of the state as "employer" and as direct appropriator of surplus. This "employer" role exposes the relationship between the state and domestic and international capital, particularly their common interest in containing the growth of the share of wage income in national output, and in increasing the surplus generated by the workforce. When this circumstance is combined with the state's obligation, as part of its economic function, to ensure "industrial peace" and "economic stability"—in its *own* industries as well as in others—the result is a number of nakedly self-serving state interventions into the system of industrial relations. However, the dialectically opposite result of this development is that as the interventionist character of the state grows, the class struggle is increasingly localized *within* the state, while at the same time the state's role as common "employer" promotes worker solidarity across racial, religious, ethnic, regional, and industrial lines. State intervention therefore has a contradictory aspect, on the one hand promoting the coercive potential of the state, while on the other hand promoting a class outlook among its common employees. What actually develops out of this depends on the concrete conditions of each country.

The *eighth* characteristic is the "crises" and "interruptions" that accompany capitalist accumulation, both internationally and nationally. Since the mid-1970s a fundamental "crisis-interruption" has been a key feature of the capitalist world economy. In the nonpetroleum-producing countries in the periphery, this has had a particularly adverse effect on the growth of national output and on the living standards of the broad masses of the population. This has compounded the on-going crisis generated by poverty and economic backwardness and has also sharpened the contradiction between the level and development of the productive forces and the social relations that characterize these societies.

Because of the importance of this conjunctural crisis in global capitalist development for the emergence of the authoritarian state, I want to specify more clearly the nature of the "crisis-interruption." In brief, the situation in the periphery demonstrates the exhaustion of both the original model of capital accumulation, based on export-oriented primary production, and the subsequent model, based on import-substituting industrialization of consumer goods (and, more recently, intermediate and some capital goods). The former colonial model had—except in the case of petroleum—more or less come to an end by the mid-1950s. The import-substitution model has been the pattern *par excellence* in the "older" peripheral capitalist societies of Latin America, as well as in some recent postcolonial societies, particularly in east Asia. A model of accumulation based on export-oriented manufacturing, in close collaboration with major transnational firms, has been a recent feature of some peripheral societies, also particularly in east Asia. No model, however, has been able to generate an autocentric pattern of growth in the periphery; and, because of the unequal development associated with capitalism, all have resulted in an ever widening gap between the economic successes of the center and those of the periphery.

At the global level, the present crisis marks the end of another long wave of capitalist expansion, lasting from 1945 to 1970. The long wave ended for many reasons, but the most fundamental are:

—The end of post-World War II U.S. hegemony in the capitalist world and the number of different growth centers that have developed in the capitalist system, in particular the European Economic Community (West Germany) and Japan.

—The rapid growth of Eastern Europe, particularly when measured in terms of its contribution to gross world output, to manufacturing, to technology, and to armaments production.

—The emergence of the oil-producing states and the impact of this on the global division of income.

—The growth of nationalist measures in the periphery, whose objective is to alter the terms of their engagement in the world division of labor.

The structural crisis of world capitalism has manifested itself in many ways: a sluggish demand for imports, international inflation, persistent balance-of-payments crises in several important capitalist countries, and the development of nationalist and "beggar-thy-neighbor" policies that have put severe pressure on international regulatory mechanisms. The generalized foreign exchange crisis and the slow growth in the demand for exports of the nonoil-producing countries of the periphery have forced a growing indebtedness (with the attendant risks of default) and restrictions on the demand for imports. These in turn have led to lower domestic consumption, a shortage of consumer goods, raw materials, spare parts, and so on, and to reduced economic production because of the high import content of domestic output and consumption. The inefficiencies of the rapidly expanding state sector in the periphery have been revealed during this crisis and have also aggravated the exploitation of the workforce.

Given all this, the ability to maintain existing patterns of internal domination rests heavily on the ability of the state to win a reduction in the growth of real wages and the standard of living of the masses, along with increased worker productivity. Without these there can be no lasting increase in the profitability of the state and private sectors. The only exceptions to this rule are the countries whose resources have increased the opportunities for them to earn monopoly rents in the world economy—i.e., those with oil. It is out of the effort to ensure increased profits and a reduced share of wages that the state is forced to restructure, and it is out of this process that an authoritarian state emerges. In other words, the crisis of the society and the world economy together engender a crisis that threatens the continuation of the regime in power, as well as the continued social and economic domination of the class and state on whose behalf it rules. It is because of this that the authoritarian state is the specific product of a conjuncture of world capitalism and peripheral capitalist development. Its imposition is the ruling-class response to the crisis confronting the society.

Methods of rule

Given the material basis of the authoritarian state, what are its principal methods of rule? In chapter 5 we saw that after independence the military, bureaucratic, and ideological apparatuses of the postcolonial state expanded rapidly. This expansion did not, of course, happen separately, but its aspects related closely, and in this interaction lies a key explanation of the methods of rule of the authoritarian state. Thus, for example, the expansion of the executive and its bureaucracy—the major organ of state autonomy—was supported by the rapid expansion of the military, particularly as popular support for the ruling regimes diminished. When increasingly unpopular regimes respond to their growing unpopularity by blocking the opposition's legal or constitutional access to power, the rapid development of the ideological apparatus is necessary in order to whip up "legitimacy" (whether in the name of "development," "national security," or whatever) for the authoritarian structure of the state. As we shall see, however, at a certain point these interactions lead to a "constitutional" restructuring of the state and the promulgation of a new "legal" structure.

Before we proceed to examine further the methods of authoritarian rule, an important methodological point must be clarified. While the authoritarian state is a historical materialist category (and so cannot and should not be confused with "authoritarianism" or tyrannical methods of rule alone), the specific methods through which the authoritarian state operates are not therefore unimportant. On the contrary, they are of great importance to the class struggle, if only because they are the most common ways in which both rulers and ruled perceive this state. One of my purposes here is to get behind this perception or appearance; nevertheless, it remains a real social consideration that a state is often perceived through its methods of rule. Therefore, while it remains true that an understanding of the material base is necessary if the deeper significance of the state mechanisms are to be understood, this undertaking is not complete without an appreciation of the methods of rule.

The most obvious of these is a highly developed system of terror and repression. Despite poverty and economic crisis, these states finance a large military apparatus.[1] As an example, while just over 6 percent of total world output is devoted to military expenditure, and while its growth is rapid in all social systems, its growth in the periphery has increased 1.5 times as fast as GNP. Indeed, in some regions (i.e., Asia) expenditure on militarization is presently higher as a percentage of GNP than what the NATO countries expend on the military and education and health. The generalization of terror and repression in these societies is linked to the use of torture, assassination, and other forms of physical violence against opponents, or would-be opponents, of the ruling classes. It is also linked to the development of a group of "political personnel" in the security services—this being an outgrowth of the ruling regime, which eventually comes to dominate these services. A deprofessionalization of the security services usually precedes the entrenchment of these "political personnel" in the repressive arm of the state. In pursuit of such objectives, the authoritarian state often shows a sophistication that far exceeds that manifested in other areas of activity. Thus, as Egbal Ahmad has aptly pointed out in a study of this type of state,

> they are even experimenting with new methods of terrorizing the people and eliminating their opposition while reducing the "visibility" of their excesses. Increasingly, people are tortured in "safe houses," in civilian quarters rather than identifiable prisons or concentration camps. Actual and potential dissenters disappear more often than they are imprisoned.[2]

As figures cited in the study demonstrate, "The scales of violence exercise credulity."[3] Over 350,000 persons were tortured by the Shah in Iran; 500,000 to 1 million Communists were killed in Indonesia after the 1965 coup; and over 30,000 persons disappeared in Latin America between 1968 and 1978.[4] Ahmad goes on:

> The purpose of governmental coercion appears to have shifted from punishment to repression. For example, torture is increasingly administered not so much to obtain information or punish a member of the opposition but literally to discourage people from linking with each other politically and socially.[5]

Significantly, this development is more marked in Third World states than in other parts of the world, indicating that the solution to a political crisis in the periphery need not follow the same lines as in the center. Indeed, in the center the preferred solution is the bourgeois-democratic state form.[6]

In the beginning openly repressive rule is usually linked to nepotism, clientelism, and other types of corruption. Corruption generally becomes entrenched in the structure of the state *and* in the structure of all other social institutions. The expansion of the state into the economy, and the accompanying growth of its bureaucracy, provides the basis for this development because it widens the scope for corrupt practices: administrative decision-making is increasingly used in the control of the society's resources—i.e., in the import-export trade, in granting production licenses, in providing state subsidies as incentives to production, and so on.

Repression in the authoritarian state operates covertly as well as overtly. Covert repression hides the excesses of the ruling regime. In an effort to develop covert forms of repression, a second set of mechanisms—police-administrative restraints on freedom—develop. Administrative decisions are used to curtail such freedoms as assembly, speech, the right to form associations, and so on. These police-administrative methods also encourage a third development, the use of private armed groups attached to the ruling apparatus. This avoids official police investigations or police surveillance of state activities. Such "death squads" operate with "unofficial" sanction, which not only affords them legal impunity but means that any attempt to resist their operations are treated by the legal arm of the state as illegal! This explains how easily such groups can attack public meetings and execute dissidents, while when those who are attacked defend themselves they are arrested and charged with using violence.

A fourth development is the growth of a large "unproductive" sector of spies, enforcers, assassins, thugs, and so on. These draw heavily on the surpluses appropriated by the state, while at the same time increasingly encouraging the orientation of state activity toward "security first." This generates a conflict between "production" and "welfare" expenditures and unproductive security expenditures.

A fifth development is growing administrative manipulation of the electoral and legal process, and of constitutionality in general. This is done to create a "legal" basis for the "unconstitutional" exercise of state power. In the former British colonies, where this development is particularly noticeable, it has been aided by the existence of a large "gray area" of constitutionality, the result of the coexistence of common law (a legacy of British colonial domination) and the written constitution. This "gray area" has been used to foster the development of the executive power of the state by advancing the legal claim that all residual powers (i.e., powers not defined in either the constitution or common law), as well as supreme power previously exercised by the colonial state, have devolved onto the chief executive of the postcolonial state rather than to the population at large. Thus the British doctrine that the "Crown can do no wrong" has been used as a cover for the arbitrary exercise of executive power—since it is presumed that all the powers of the Crown have devolved to the local state.

A sixth development is that the authoritarian state has had to destroy the organizations of the masses in order to assure its own security. This has meant concentrated attacks on the trade unions, on opposition political parties, and on any means of public communication—newspapers, radio and television stations—not directly under the control of the state. The need to do this is all the more urgent because the political groups that dominate the state do not have a mass following to support them—their main internal support coming from the armed forces.

A final important development is the emergence of what might be called "parallel institutions." Here the state either sponsors new "private" organizations (i.e., trade unions, church groups) that parallel existing mass organizations, or takes over existing ones (i.e., trade unions, professional associations, and so on). By manipulating state patronage and conducting fraudulent elections, these government-sponsored organizations very quickly become official and legally recognized, and, given the extensive state control over employment, resources, and so on, the speed is not surprising. Such an indirect approach avoids the protest that the state is destroying the mass organizations and also divides the supporters of these existing organizations that are under attack by the state.

The combination of the mechanisms of rule discussed here and the material conditions promoting their development discussed previously make the authoritarian state a different form of postcolonial state. Thus there is no "succession" of one government by another (either through constitutional or unconstitutional means), but the substitution of a new form of state— a situation not dissimilar from the origins of the fascist state in the developed capitalist formations of Europe.

The international context

The authoritarian state is not a purely national or local phenomenon. It is not exclusively the product of internal, autonomous, national development within a peripheral capitalist society. Indeed, as noted above, the specific point at which the authoritarian state appears with increasing frequency in the periphery is a time of a structural crisis of accumulation in the capitalist world economy as a whole which compounds the on-going crises of poverty, economic backwardness, and underdeveloped class structures. Given the way in which the periphery is integrated into world capitalism and given its dependence on the international bourgeoisie for investment funds, markets, technology, finance, goods, etc., links between the local and international structures of authoritarianism are fundamental to the development of authoritarianism in the periphery. More specifically, these links are based on the alliance between the local ruling classes in the periphery and those in the capitalist center countries.

In general, therefore, the local structures of authoritarianism will be reinforced by the international structures of domination. This is plainly revealed in the role imperialism plays in arming these regimes, in providing them with sophisticated methods of internal surveillance, and in training personnel to work in the coercive structures of the state. The continuous upgrading of the military and counterinsurgency apparatuses is too well known to need repeating in detail. The reinforcement of local authoritarianism does not, however, rely solely on support for the local armed forces—despite its undoubted importance.

Two other aspects of support are also of fundamental importance. One takes the form of economic aid and finance (bilaterally, regionally, and internationally). The IMF and World Bank, together with U.S. and European bilateral (and in some cases regional) support for these regimes is crucial to their continued existence. Not surprisingly, then, there is a direct correlation between U.S. aid and human rights violations, as Noam Chomsky and Edward Herman have pointed out: "For most of the sample countries United States-controlled aid has been positively related to investment climate and inversely related to the maintenance of a democratic order and human rights."[7] Similarly, Michael Klare has shown that between 1973 and 1977 the ten principal recipients of U.S. economic and military aid had the ten worst human rights records, as determined by internationally recognized human rights organizations.[8] These ten countries received $4.3 billion economic and military aid, and spent $18.2 billion on U.S.-supplied arms—purchases that accounted for 37 percent of all U.S. weapons sales!

The second aspect of support is ideological. Its principal features are highly publicized references to the negative consequences of a Communist takeover, anti-Soviet and anti-Cuban propaganda, and an appeal for "stability" and a suitable "investment climate" in order to attract capital from overseas. In the face of a shortage of domestic capital these appeals are very persuasive, and also provide the justification for beefing up the repressive forces, both in the center and the periphery.

In conclusion, it is important to note that the local authoritarian state is not only supported by the international structures of domination but *cannot exist without them.* Further, while the bourgeoisies in the center have been forced by their own working classes to accept the bourgeois-democratic form of the state, and indeed now propagandize it as the particular virtue of capitalist development, they nevertheless readily support authoritarian state forms in the periphery. This position is indeed necessary if they are to maintain the particular option that they now exercise in the center. In other words, the center's ability to appropriate output from the periphery (with which to satisfy its own exploited classes) is contingent on the underdevelopment of the bourgeoisie in the periphery and on the prevention of a revolutionary transformation of political relations and state power in favor of the workers and peasants in these countries.

Some concluding comments

In conclusion, the description and analysis of the authoritarian state can be supplemented by a few further general observations. First, in some countries there are deeply embedded cultural traditions that reinforce authoritarian patterns of rule. Thus, as we saw earlier, the plantation structure of the Caribbean has worked against the development of cultural traditions of democratic or representative rule, and of political participation in social life. Historically, in fact, dictatorial forms have been the rule rather than the exception. In such situations, the development of authoritarian methods of rule in part reflects the historical tendency for these states to put "politics in command." Such a tendency has fostered the depoliticization of the community and negated many of the positive features of the development of mass politics, particularly the growth of mass political organizations during the immediate pre-independence period, and the growth and development of trade unions and other worker organizations. As H. Goulbourne has observed in connection with the demobilization of the trade union movement in postcolonial societies (in this case in Africa),

> generally speaking, organized labor, which had joined forces with the nationalist party in the independence struggle, was blamed for threatening an apparent unity by making legitimate demands for workers. This was generally interpreted as a threat by those who held state power and who wished to use this power to provide the dominant classes with secure economic bases.[9]

This depoliticization of the community has invariably weakened the defenses of the masses and promoted the consolidation of authoritarian tendencies.

A second observation is that the authoritarian state *can develop with either a "left" or "right" posture.* While I am loathe to use these terms (and in the next section I shall argue that states cannot be termed "progressive," "socialist," "Marxist," or "left" on the basis of self-advertised claims), the social fact is that these types are distinguished in common parlance. But insofar as the leaders of these states cannot hide their authoritarian character, this supports the argument that the roots of this state form go deeper than the level of ideology or of the consciousness of the rulers. Again, however, a word of caution. In taking this position I am not ignoring the different lines of development implicit in the two ideological rationalizations. The "left" ideology expounds on the need to develop self-reliant economies with a strong noncapitalist and anti-imperialist orientation. The insistence of the ruling section of the petty bourgeoisie on ideological conformity to "African socialism" or "Arab socialism" or "cooperative socialism," and the elimination of opposition parties and of any possibility of a legal and constitutional change of government, is justified on the ground that this national ideology is paramount. Bourgeois democracy is dismissed as irrelevant in the existing situation. The "right" ideology is that stability, law and order, and freedom from subversion are necessary to secure a suitable investment climate for indigenous private capital. State investment, where it occurs, is necessary to speed up the process of capitalist transformation.

Thirdly, while the authoritarian state may appear to be a solution to the crisis facing the ruling classes in these countries, more often than not this state form actually *intensifies* the political crisis and reduces the ability of these states to promote stable and expanded reproduction. The authoritarian state is at best an unstable state form and, if not overthrown in a popular uprising, degenerates further along the lines of military rule and dictatorship. This degeneration does not make a solution for the ruling classes any more likely, and in fact is a further manifestation of the deepening crisis and the increasing need for a social revolution based on socialism *and* democracy in the periphery.

To what can we attribute the instability of the authoritarian state? To begin with, while authoritarianism seeks a closer and closer equating of state power and class power, conflicts persist between these two arenas of social power, and the authoritarian manner in which the state seeks to resolve these conflicts in its favor often exaggerates the political consequences of this state intervention, thereby *negating* the very tendency toward equating state power and class power. Intimidation, the arbitrary use of state power in issuing import licenses, the punitive administration of tax laws, and so on, are used to win conformity to the designs of the state. Not infrequently, however, this exercise of state power only succeeds in terrifying other sections of the ruling petty bourgeoisie (top bureaucrats, local businesspeople, professionals, etc.) and alienating them from political power.

Another source of instability is that the growing equation of class power and state power partially reflects the progressive narrowing of the class base of the state, as a smaller and smaller section of the petty bourgeoisie feels its interests are represented in such a state. The fact that the ruling group does not have a highly developed mass base intensifies the tendency for its support among the propertied classes to narrow.

Finally, the use of open force, systematic repression, and the violation of human rights invariably makes the state increasingly unpopular, even as it takes on the appearance of greater and greater invincibility. This unpopularity potentially broadens the opposition and eventually leads to open rebellion. At this stage civil war is imminent.

It is necessary to bear in mind the important consideration that the authoritarian state is not the preferred solution of either the dominant classes or strata or even of the political leadership. It is therefore not a universal solution even at this conjuncture, as the existence of other types of state clearly shows. It is one solution, albeit a highly probable one. The state, after all, is the institutionalization of class conflicts and antagonisms, and to the extent that it loses legitimacy, and the consent of the governed, it reduces its own ability to resolve social conflicts peacefully and without open resort to force. When force is resorted to, the coercive character of the state, and the fact that it has been imposed by the dominant classes, is more easily perceived by the masses.

In the years of European fascism this point was clearly demonstrated. From the point of view of the developed capitalist countries, bourgeois-democratic rule has been the most "successful" form of the capitalist state and the ruling class in these countries has an interest—a real interest, as distinct from a tactical propaganda interest—in its preservation. In the peripheral capitalist countries, however, there is no such historical experience. The colonial experience was one of nonparticipatory, nondemocratic, nonrepresentational politics. It would take tremendous vision for the representatives of the ruling petty bourgeoisie to recognize the long-run advantage of perpetuating the domination of its forms of capital with the "consent" of labor—and it is too preoccupied with its own immediate interests to generate such a vision. Add to this the social atmosphere that makes it relatively easy to rationalize authoritarian rule and its prevalence can be better appreciated.

In conclusion I would like to reiterate a point made in the first chapter: the form of the state has a grave effect on the future prospects of the dominated classes. The choice between the authoritarian state and a more parliamentary bourgeois-democratic orientation is a very significant choice in terms of the advance of the working class and peasantry. Experience in the countries of the periphery shows that the development of worker and other mass organizations depends on belief that these have the democratic right to exist. Where the state is of the authoritarian type this right is denied, and political confrontations are immediately translated into physical confrontations. A war of liberation from the dictatorship (a national offensive) or a coup eventually become the only options for any governmental succession. This explains not only the frequency of coups in the periphery, but the political strategy of broad-based national fronts against a dictator. I shall return to this point in the final chapter.

Socialism and democracy in the periphery

These points lead us directly to the question of the relevance of political democracy to peripheral societies. First it is necessary to be clear as to the meaning of political democracy in this context. Here the term includes the following commonly accepted practices:

(1) The absence of any discrimination on the grounds of race, religion, tribe, property/income, political party affiliation, etc., in the exercise of political opinion, whether expressed directly or through an elected representative.

(2) Except for stipulations on the legal age of voting, all citizens have an equal vote. All persons are allowed to vote according to their own opinion, and may support freely and without discrimination the political party of their choice.

(3) All political parties have equal status before the law, so that a contest between organized political groups is a real contest, representing real alternatives.

(4) The principles of majority rule hold in the election of representatives and in the legislative process. A majority decision, however, does not limit the minority's right to become a legal and constitutional majority.

(5) Due process operates in the legal system to ensure that the above rights are enforced.

While the above may not exhaust the meaning of representative or political democracy, the *absence* of any of these practices violates the fundamentals of representative democracy; such a society is by definition not democratic.

This formulation has two notable exclusions, both of which are deliberate. First, political democracy is confined to what are traditionally described as "bourgeois-democratic rights." It does not include social and economic rights, without which much of the significance of the above is reduced. But since these rights are impossible to achieve in a capitalist formation, whether developed or peripheral, and since their absence constitutes one of the main social factors impelling change in a socialist direction, their omission is deliberate. Its implications will be expanded upon below. Second, such democratic rights as workers' self-management, rank-and-file democracy, guild socialism, or the Leninist concept of the "soviets" are also omitted, again because they are impossible within the framework of capitalist relations, and in any case while they may be complementary to representative democratic institutions, they can be no substitute for them.

The omission of these two areas of democracy—vital though they are—thus springs from the belief that capitalism, whether of the developed or peripheral sort, cannot generate the socioeconomic conditions that the establishment of these rights presupposes. Political and representative democracy in this wider sense cannot survive and grow without the eventual transformation of the socioeconomic conditions of the vast majority of the world's population. In this sense, therefore, the struggle for political democracy is vital to the struggle for socialism. One cannot exist without the other. Obvious as it seems, this position is only now coming to be accepted. For too long, many on the left have counterposed "socialism" to "political democracy," arguing that political democracy is a bourgeois illusion that masks the reality of the economic and social domination of workers by capitalists. While there is truth in this, there is none in the next step of the argument, which is that the "dictatorship of the proletariat" is essential for socialist development, and that this dictatorship can encompass (supposedly inter-mediate) dictatorial forms of rule. The fact is, as I have pointed out elsewhere, that the ideological basis of this attitude lies either in an elementary misunderstanding of the notion "dic-tatorship of the proletariat" or in a deliberate distortion of Marxism. Anyone who has read Marx knows that the term "dic-tatorship of the proletariat" refers to the sociological domina-tion of the working class. This domination does not encompass any such trite and superficial political notion as authoritarian or tyrannical government. The sociological domination of the working class is expressed in its domination over the means of production and its direction of the labor process. It can also, contrary to this belief, be expressed in a democratic trans-formation.[10]

While this view is increasingly accepted in the center coun-tries—as can be seen in the debates on Eurocommunism and the "British road to socialism"—there is an altogether embar-rassing silence as regards the periphery. Yet so-called bourgeois freedoms, which in the periphery are dismissed as "luxuries" (thus providing the rationalization for their constant abuse) include such fundamental rights as freedom of speech and expression, freedom of association, freedom of publication, the right to privacy, the right to representative institutions, and so on. These rights have everywhere been achieved only after heroic mass struggles. In the developed capitalist formations, working-class struggle has been the instrument for achieving these rights, even though there, more than in the periphery, they coincided with the ruling class's long-run conception of right and fairness in the political order. In the periphery they have not been the product of colonial or imperialist generosity, or of the benevolence of the local ruling classes, but the result of mass struggles.

In the developed capitalist formations the democratic trans-formation of the state has generally been achieved. In the peripheral capitalist formations, however, the same is not true, and the rise of the authoritarian state has often helped advance this issue to the forefront of political struggle. In some countries—El Salvador, Guyana, Iran under the Shah—the principal contradiction is between those who control the state and *all* the classes and groups that are excluded, including certain sections of the economically dominant classes. Yet even in this situation, as if with an eye to the future, the classes sustaining the struggle for democracy (as was the case with the struggle for liberation from colonial rule) are the working class and the peasantry, while the main supporters of the ruling regimes are the reactionary segments of the locally based international bourgeoisie. It is also true that sections of the politically dominant petty bourgeoisie both support these regimes *and* participate in antidictatorial alliances against them, but the key point is that political democracy in the periphery is limited to a far greater degree than is necessitated by the underdevelopment of capitalism in these societies and that its absence cannot be explained or excused by this consideration.

Before we leave this point, two further features of political democracy under capitalism should be noted. The first is that while political democracy increases the scope for the advance of the working class or the masses, it does not—and indeed cannot—*guarantee* it. Further, even when it does lead to some advance, the workers and the masses cannot alter their status in the society without altering class and legal relations—and hence the class basis of state. Second, until and unless the workers achieve just such a transformation of class relations, their political freedoms remain insecure. Experience has shown, beginning with the Soviet revolution and continuing down to the present, that if the capitalists and imperialists believe that their class domination is threatened because of a growing political awareness on the part of the working class, they will not hesitate to demolish freedom and political democracy and maintain capitalist rule by tyranny. In other words, democracy is both a *danger* and a *tool* for the ruling class, and how democratic practice finally develops depends on the concrete circumstances of the political struggle. There is, therefore, a dialectical relation between political democracy and socialism, because not only is the state of the class struggle primary, but the class struggle in the periphery cannot be separated from the state of working-class democracy and participation in national life. The advance of socialism therefore depends on the effective advance of the working class *throughout* society.

The position outlined here is not the same as the position taken in the debate over democratic forms by some Western European Communist parties (i.e., France, Spain, Italy) because the contexts differ. Capitalist development in Western Europe has raised the level of development of the productive forces to its present heights, while the bourgeois-democratic transformation of political life (as symbolized in the "theoretic-legal equality of all in law and political life") has been achieved. Thus although this equality is limited by class inequality, the state is nevertheless forced to function as if the presumption in favor of certain political and social rights and practices were real and effective. This is a real working-class gain. In this situation it would be impossible for a Western European Marxist party to have a program for building socialism that does not explicitly recognize the degree of development of bourgeois-democratic forms and practices. In the periphery, however, this condition does not hold, so that the context of the debate differs fundamentally. In the periphery democratic political forms are insecurely established, so that the struggle is to entrench them, while at the same time seeking advances on other socio-economic fronts.

There is a long Marxist tradition, beginning with Marx himself, that supports the position I am taking on the relationship of any future socialism and democracy. This is what Rosa Luxemburg had to say on the Russian Revolution:

> Freedom only for the supporters of the government, only for the members of one party—however numerous they may be—is no freedom at all. Freedom is always and exclusively freedom for the one who thinks differently. Not because of any fanatical concept of "justice" but because all that is instructive, wholesome, and purifying in political freedom depends on this essential characteristic, and its effectiveness vanishes when "freedom" becomes a special privilege.

She goes on to warn:

> The public life of countries with limited freedom is so poverty stricken, so miserable, so rigid, so unfruitful, precisely because through the exclusion of democracy, it cuts off the living sources of all spiritual riches and progress. . . . Public control is indispensably necessary. Otherwise, the exchange of experiences remains only within the closed circle of the officials of the new regime. Corruption becomes inevitable . . . with the repression of political life in the land as a whole, life in the soviets must also become more and more crippled. Without general elections, without unrestricted freedom of press and assembly, without a free struggle of opinion, life dies out in every public institution, becomes a mere semblance of life, in which only the bureaucracy remains as an active element. Public life gradually falls asleep, a few dozen party leaders of inexhaustible energy and boundless experience direct and rule. Among them, in reality only a dozen outstanding heads do the leading and an elite of the working class is invited from time to time to meetings where they are to applaud the speeches of the leaders, and to approve proposed resolutions unanimously—at bottom, then, a clique affair—a dictatorship, to be sure, not the dictatorship of the proletariat, however, but only the dictatorship of a handful of politicians.

Moving from warning to practical advice, she points out:

> Socialist democracy is not something which begins only in the promised land after the foundations of socialist economy are created; . . . [it] begins simultaneously with the destruction of class rule and the construction of socialism . . . this dictatorship consists in the *manner of applying democracy*, not in its elimination, . . . this dictatorship must be the work of a *class* and not of a leading minority in the name of the class—that is, it must proceed step by step out of the active participation of the masses.[11]

These long quotes show that the points made above are central to the mainstream of Marxism. A number of theoreticians within the Marxist tradition are today coming to accept this position. Thus N. Bobbio has observed:

> The error [of separating socialism from representative democracy] stems from the belief that the citizen has no problems distinct from those of the workers (or the producer). But these

problems do exist. They are precisely the problems of civil and political liberties, whose underemphasis, sometimes mixed with derision, mockery, or downright scorn, is unfortunately one of the undesirable inheritances of Marxist thought. The basic text of this tradition is a few pages from the *Jewish Question*, which has become a convenient license for all aspiring dictators (with or without the proletariat). The abuse is all the more serious in that the current interpretation, which turns a few pages of that writing into a kind of counter-declaration of the rights of man, goes beyond the intention and deep meaning of that essay, whose central incontrovertible thesis is that political emancipation is not all of human emancipation.[13]

Nicos Poulantzas, one of the foremost recent contributors to the development of the Marxist theory of the state, has also noted:

This much we know already: socialism cannot be democratic here and of another kind over there. The concrete situation may of course differ, and the strategies undoubtedly have to be adapted to the country's specific features. But democratic socialism is the only kind possible.[13]

Later he makes the same point again: "One thing is certain: socialism will be democratic or it will not be at all."[14]

Arguing that democracy and socialism are necessarily related does not mean that the struggle for socialism is any easier. What it does is raise the real danger of a "social-democratic" transformation of the working-class struggle. This danger can only be overcome by a political practice that takes the mass movement beyond this option. To remove the danger by removing political democracy is to pave the way for some other dictatorship than that of the proletariat. In conclusion, therefore, we can agree with Poulantzas that:

Risks there are, although they are no longer quite where they used to be: at worst, we could be heading for camps and massacres as appointed victims. But to that I reply: if one weighs up the risks, that is in any case preferable to massacring other people only to end up ourselves beneath the blade of a Committee of Public Safety of some dictator of the proletariat.[15]

Classical fascism and the authoritarian state

At this point it is useful to examine the key features of the classic fascist state and the Latin American "bureaucratic-authoritarian" state in order to highlight how they differ from the authoritarian state as presented here.

The authoritarian state is a new sociopolitical category and not simply a variant of the classic fascist state. The reasons for the difference are straightforward. The classic fascist state cannot, any more than the authoritarian state, be simply defined as tyrannical or dictatorial rule; it too must be located in a specific structural and historical context—otherwise fascism, and the fascist state, would be reduced to a historical and apolitical category. This is exactly what the classic definition of fascism—the definition arrived at by the 13th Plenum of the Executive Committee in February 1934 sought to avoid—it defined fascism as "the open dictatorship of the most reactionary, most chauvinistic, and most imperialist elements of finance capital." In his political report to the 7th Congress of the Communist International, Dimitrov went on to identify an important feature of classic fascism:

> The accession to power of fascism is not an ordinary succession of one bourgeois government by another, but a substitution of one state form of class domination of the bourgeoisie—bourgeois democracy—by another form—open terrorist dictatorship.

The classic definition located fascism in a specific historical and structural context. It saw it occuring at a conjucture when:

(1) Imperialism was faced with an economic collapse of global proportions. This economic collapse was fueled by the effects of World War I, the intensified interimperialist commercial rivalry as the world market contracted, and the unprecedented manifestations of inflation, financial crisis, and unemployment that accompanied efforts to overcome this crisis.

(2) There was a strong popular offensive against bourgeois rule in the face of an assault on the standard of living. This political offensive was fueled by the success of the October Revolution, which served to generate among the ruling classes

the specter of a "Communist takeover." The "red menace" had become a "real menace."

(3) The generalized crisis made it possible for the most reactionary elements of the bourgeoisie to dominate state power and so seek to impose their version of a "national" solution on behalf of the whole class.

Certain features of the fascist state follow from the above, and show how it differs from the authoritarian state. *First*, while the fascist state emerged in a developed capitalist formation with a hegemonic class, the authoritarian state emerges in an underdeveloped capitalist formation with no clear hegemonic class, and with the ruling class's influence over the state highly conjectural and fluid. In fascism the bourgeoisie is generally forced to surrender its historically acquired influence over the state (as well as its insistence on the bourgeois-democratic form of state power), to its most reactionary elements, in the belief that in their hands the state, and only the state, can solve the political, social, and economic crises confronting the class as a whole. At this point in time the most reactionary fraction of the bourgeoisie becomes the dominant element within the class.

Second, in fascism the crisis confronting the ruling class was not only national but international in its dimensions. It was a crisis of imperialism, and rivalry among the major nationally constituted bourgeoisies was a key factor—the scramble for markets and the "beggar-thy-neighbor" commercial and credit policies pursued by the European powers between World War I and World War II are well known. This rivalry not only contributed to the development of the crisis, but intensified as the crisis unfolded. On the other hand, while the crisis that gives rise to the development of the authoritarian state is also international in scope, its circumstances differ in two important ways. One is that the developed capitalist formations have painfully learned from the experience of the 1930s the self-defeating consequences of the pursuit of national advantage in times of rapidly declining global economic activity, and have instead sought to harmonize national, regional, and international economic policies. The second is that while the ruling class under fascism was made up of relatively independent elements in the international structure of imperialism, and while this relative independence is strengthened today—as can be seen in the extent to which coordinated national efforts to overcome crises have become the order of the day in developed capitalist states—the ascendant national and petty bourgeoisie in the authoritarian state has a *dependent* role within the international structure of imperialism and can have little effective influence over crises at the international level. The development of authoritarian solutions is in some measure a direct consequence of this dependency relation.

Third, while fascism occurred in societies with comparatively highly developed levels of productive forces where market relations, particularly the labor market, had become generalized, the societies in which the authoritarian state emerges are characterized by the underdevelopment of the productive forces and the absence of market relations in many sectors of the economy. Under fascism, attacks on worker organizations had two objectives: one was to defeat the workers politically and to reduce the strength of popular resistance; the other was to follow up this defeat by pursuing the militarization of labor—that is, the *negation* of labor market relations. The ruling classes believed that this was necessary in order to reduce production costs, and to raise productivity and profit rates. In the authoritarian state, on the other hand, while the political defeat of the working class is also the prime objective, the solution is not seen in the militarization of labor and the elimination of the labor market. The politically dominant groups in the periphery do not believe that the resolution of the economic crisis lies within their national capabilities, and so lean heavily on forms of collaboration with international capital and the transnational firm in order to generate economic expansion. They are therefore forced to see their task as requiring the *expansion* of capitalist relations in order to attract foreign capital (including a well-organized labor market) and thus avoid the formation of command-type labor structures.

Fourth, while both the fascist and authoritarian states undergo a restructuring, and while neither is the result of an "ordinary succession" from one government to another but are the result of the "substitution" of a new state form, the substitution of the fascist state took place when two important features of state and political relations existed which do not affect the authoritarian state. One is that there was already a considerable fusion of state and monopoly capital in fascist societies. While the state plays a major, and often dominant, role in economic reproduction in some peripheral capitalist formations, the fusion of the interests of state and private capital is not of the same order as that associated with the fusion of state and monopoly interests in Europe at the time of the rise of fascism. In Europe, not only did monopoly exist as a market form, but the major monopoly firms were important independent and autonomous sources of accumulation and technical advance. Monopolies in the periphery do not have these characteristics. The other important feature is that state restructuring under fascism took place *after* the bourgeois-democratic revolution and *after* bourgeois democracy as a form of bourgeois rule had been accepted. In the case of the authoritarian state, on the other hand, a bourgeois-democratic transformation has not yet been achieved.

Fifth, in classic European fascism there were large social layers—i.e., the petty bourgeoisie, the unemployed, demobilized soldiers, etc.—that were molded into party organizations in support of fascist rule and that were distinguished by their hierarchical structure. In the case of the authoritarian state, however, the ruling group does not have such a mass base, although it may try in corporatist fashion to create one or to manipulate those in existence. Sometimes there is not even a mass party, and power is maintained through the more or less open use of force.

Sixth, and finally, the ideology of nationalism plays a particular role in the development of fascism. In the fascist state the ruling class exploited the social, psychological, and cultural prejudices of ethnocentrism and nationalism. The starting point of this ideology was the claim of cultural and moral superiority over other nations and groups. But, as I shall show in more detail in the next chapter, while ideology plays a central role in the perpetuation of the authoritarian state, the lines it takes reflect important differences in the historical and cultural situation. "Law and order," "social integration," "anti-communism," "development," and "socialism" are the labels through which the propaganda of the authoritarian state work. Even where racial, ethnic, religious, or cultural minorities are being obliterated, such obliteration is rarely openly and directly advanced in national terms. In part this reflects real differences in the levels of education and social consciousness today as compared to the 1930s.

In concluding this comparison, it is important to repeat once again that the fascist state, like the authoritarian state, was not necessarily the *preferred* solution of the ruling class. As those who have studied the fascism of the interwar years have shown, fascism developed in Italy and Germany but other solutions were attempted elsewhere. It is important to remember this if we are to avoid a mechanical application of the hypotheses advanced here.[16]

Latin American bureaucratic authoritarianism and the authoritarian state

There is a large and diverse literature on the bureaucratic-authoritarian state and corporatism in Latin America. Its central ideas can be summarized briefly as follows:[17]

(1) Where military rule follows upon a coup—i.e., Argentina and Brazil—the military rules as an *institution* rather than as individual military persons. In all major organizations the military has decisive weight.

(2) Institutionalized military rule is combined with a "technocratic, bureaucratic approach to policymaking (as opposed to a more 'political' approach through which policies are shaped by economic and political demands from different sectors of society, expressed through such channels as elections, legislatures, political parties and labor unions)."[18] This technocratic approach allows for the incorporation of civilian technocrats into the economic apparatus.

(3) While there is institutionalized military rule, and a bureaucratic approach to state policy, the state's principal social base is the upper bourgeoisie, i.e., "the upper fractions of a highly oligopolized and transnationalized bourgeoisie."[19]

(4) The crisis that finally gives birth to this state has two main dimensions. First, there is an economic impasse which

the society reaches when the "easy" phase of import-substitution industrialization is at an end. (The "easy" phase refers to the simple assembly of imported inputs for the production of consumer goods for the urban high-income market, with low backward linkages to the national economy, behind strong tariffs and direct barriers to imports.) There is limited internal control of the quality, consumer financing, servicing, and pricing of these goods. The economic impasse is punctuated by persistent balance-of-payments crises, inflation, the intensification of the struggle for a piece of the economic pie, and emerging income inequalities. At this point changes in public policy are called for, in particular export promotion, a "deepening" of industrialization through the production of intermediate and capital goods in order to create the necessary internal linkages with the consumer goods sector, revised tax structures and the creation of an efficient capital market, a greater reliance on market forces, and a greater emphasis on science and technology. These policies require a structural change in the economic function of the state. Second, the international system creates continuous crises in the process of accumulation at the global level and these intensify the problems posed by the economic impasse. Mass unrest, and in particular an offensive by labor, creates a threat to the capitalist "parameters" of the state. The military coup is a response to this threat, and the subsequent repression of the populace and liquidation of political democracy are designed to reassert capitalist supremacy and "depoliticize" social issues by dealing with them in terms of the supposedly "neutral" and "objective" criteria of economic rationality.[20]

A number of considerations immediately spring to mind. First, the bureaucratic-authoritarian state as developed in Latin America is a phenomenon of former colonies with a long enough period of independence to permit the significant formation of indigenous social classes of the sort that can also be found in the developed capitalist countries. Despite these states' "dependent" characteristics, there is a relatively developed bourgeoisie, which, as point (3) above indicates, forms the economic power base of the state. In addition, the landed bourgeoisie is also relatively well developed, while the development of import-substitution industrialization has created a substantially larger proletariat than in the recent postcolonial societies. Further, the longer time period has meant, in general, that far fewer nonclass factors mediate class relations (although they still remain important in certain areas, i.e., Indian/non-Indian relations in Bolivia, Mexico, Guatemala, etc.).

A second consideration is that the much longer period of independence has meant a longer period in which to struggle to consolidate sovereignty in the international arena. This, together with the previous point, means that in Latin America the "projects" of the main classes are much further advanced than in the recent postcolonial societies, as the dominance of the intermediate strata in the latter shows.

A third consideration is that while in Latin American societies the military is the dominant institution in charge of the state, this is not characteristic of the authoritarian state. Here the military apparatuses are highly developed, but they do not *take command* of the executive and ideological apparatuses. In the bureaucratic-authoritarian state, this feature means that there is often no political party around which state power is built. In the authoritarian state, on the other hand, despite the "clique" characteristics of the intermediate strata and the progressive depoliticization of the community at large, a political party of some sort does center around the leadership of the state. This makes the authoritarian state's approach to the internal crises less technocratic and more political (i.e., through the manipulation of legality and constitutionality, of the legislature and courts, and so on) than is the case in Latin America.

In both cases the conjuncture of the international and national crises is an important factor in the emergence of the particular state form. The crisis, however, differs in important regards. For example, the longer period of independence in Latin America has allowed the process of import substitution to be carried further, so that the classes associated with it are much more fully developed.[21] In addition, in some instances (i.e., Brazil) there is also a significant development of heavy industry and the export of important manufactures and technologies (motor cars, aircraft, gasahol technology, etc.). This phase of economic expansion is linked to the further development of the domestic bourgeoisie.

Finally, the crisis in Latin America has brought much more rapidly to the fore the issue of the limits to the functioning of the capitalist state in the periphery. These limits have an important influence on the ideology of these states and their position in the global system—their preoccupation with national security, anticommunism, etc. In recent postcolonial states, on the other hand, the independence period has meant that such issues as sovereignty, economic independence, national unity, and so on seem far more important than do the global struggles between capitalism and socialism. The exception is where strategic location may propel a recent postcolonial society into the heart of struggle between the "superpowers"; in that case the "East-West" conflict determines state function at almost every level.

8. Ideology and the Authoritarian State

One final task remains in our analysis of the authoritarian state: to explore the mechanisms by which the rulers seek to win "acceptance." All ruling classes attempt to develop an ideology to sustain their domination, and the case at hand is no exception. But before we examine the relationship of ideology to the authoritarian state, it is necessary to outline the major features of ideology as I shall interpret it. I shall do this in the first section, and then apply the results to the authoritarian state in the following sections.

On ideology

Marxist theory has always recognized that ideology plays a central role in the maintenance of ruling-class hegemony. The classic formulation of this position is:

> For each new class which puts itself in the place of one ruling before it, is compelled, merely in order to carry through its aim, to represent its interest as the common interest of all the members of society, that is, expressed in ideal form: it has to give its ideas the form of universality, and represent them as the only rational, universally valid ones.[1]

Further:

> The ideas of the ruling class are in every epoch the ruling ideas, i.e. the class which is the ruling *material* force of society, is at the same time its ruling *intellectual* force. The class which has the means of material production at its disposal, has control at the same time over the means of mental production, so that thereby, generally speaking, the ideas of those who lack the means of mental production, are subject to it.[2]

113

Although these quotes are justifiably famous for their forceful-
ness, it has been argued that they overstate the case, particularly with reference to those societies where private sector
production is by far the largest sphere of social activity. I
shall return to this point later, but I first want to make three
observations in this classic formulation. First, implicit in the
formulation is an analytical distinction between periods of
"revolutionary change" and periods "in between." In the former, the dominant function of ideology is "revolutionary" insofar as it seeks to overthrow the old order and expose—and
hence nullify—the ruling ideas of the old. In this context a
"revolutionary" period does not refer simply to a change in
government or regime, unless it has been produced by, and is
associated with, a revolutionary realignment of class forces
within the society. In the latter, the dominant function of ideology is to maintain and consolidate the position of the existing
ruling classes. (This does not, however, mean that "revolutionary" ideologies associated with the subordinated and
dominated classes of the society cannot coexist with the "in-
between" ideology.)

The second observation is that there is also implicit in the
formulation the view that insofar as the ruling class uses ideology to maintain its hegemony, it has the same objectives as in
its use of the state. If this is so, then it is as essential to understand the class character of ruling-class ideology as it is to
understand the class nature of the state, if we are to understand
how capitalist society functions. In other words, the inherent
complementarity of state and ideological relations must be recognized, both in terms of their nature and function: both serve
the same ends and both operate in the same sphere of public
activity. As J. McMurty aptly put it:

> Ideology and the state are for Marx neatly complementary in both
> their nature and their function. One is public ideas (ideology).
> The other is public institutions (the state). Together, they make
> up one whole, the public realm. This is how they are complemen-
> tary in nature. On the other hand, both serve one end, to protect
> the underlying ruling class economic order from change—
> ideology by concealing it, the state by enforcing it. This is how
> they show their complementarity in function. Hence Marx some-
> times refers to them as an integrated unity, as a "whole immense

superstructure": the ideas and the institution of one great public domain serving one great function, to maintain the ruling-class economic structure and its "law of motion" of surplus-value extraction intact.[3]

This complementarity in the nature and function of state and ideological relations is geared toward supporting ruling-class efforts at minimizing the use of direct force against the population, while maintaining its domination.

The third observation is that because ideology refers to a more or less coherent and integrated system of views, propositions, ideas, and so on, which together constitute a "world view," then ideology cannot be analytically separated from such other forms of social consciousness as tradition, social psychology, and the ordinary everyday consciousness that people apply to their activities. As a social category these forms of social consciousness refer to the variety of ways of feeling, thought, expression, etc., which characterize people in a given society. Their importance in shaping class outlook and class action cannot be underestimated. Unfortunately, apart from Gramsci's work, this area has been inadequately treated in Marxist analysis.[4]

The diverse feelings, thoughts, expressions, and so on which people apply to their activities are accumulated over centuries and form a part of every society's inheritance. In each new historical epoch this social inheritance is influenced by new thoughts, feelings, and outlooks that emerge in the course of social development; some of these alter old outlooks (although generally much more slowly than other areas of social change), while others reinforce them or alter their outward appearance. In class society, all forms of social consciousness are invariably influenced by, and in turn help to influence, the characteristic behavior of a class. Since, however, class societies constitute systems of domination, these forms of social consciousness generally reinforce existing patterns of domination. Thus, for example, as Marx pointed out, with the emergence of commodity production the commodity itself became a means of reinforcing domination:

A commodity is therefore a mysterious thing, simply because in it the social character of man's labour appears to them as an objective character stamped upon the product of that labour; because the relation of the producers to the sum total of their own labour is presented to them as a social relation, existing not between themselves, but between the products of their labour. . . . There it is a definite social relation between men, that assumes, in their eyes, the fantastic form of a relation between things. . . . This fetishism of commodities has its origin . . . in the peculiar social character of the labour that produces them.[5]

Although in class societies forms of social consciousness generally operate so as to ensure the prevailing system of domination, social consciousness is not only "conservative." In every class society, as I pointed out above, there coexist progressive, dissenting, "revolutionary" collections of views, thoughts, and feelings which use as their point of reference the interests of the subordinated classes. That is why in capitalist societies, developed and peripheral alike, with their developed modes of communication, struggles are always being waged to influence the consciousness of the majority of the population. These struggles take place in the institutions (church, school, media, unions, etc.) that sustain and express them.

The fourth and final observation is that while all states must try to assure their own legitimation, and use the dissemination of ruling-class ideology and the manipulation of other forms of social consciousness to do this, the practitioners of the ruling class/state functions are not always conscious of the roles they play. In other words, there is no conspiracy theory implicit in this view of the role of ideology. As in many other areas of social life, a considerable element of self-deception and false consciousness prevails and there is no doubt that many propagandists of ruling-class ideology sincerely believe their ideology to be true—that it represents a scientific interpretation of social reality. This does not, of course, rule out the existence of those so-called hacks who deliberately and consciously set out to rationalize ruling-class interests as eternal wisdom and justice. The role of these hacks varies from society to society, but is generally greatest in those states where the most thought is put into the dissemination of ruling-class ideology and the manipulation of other forms of social consciousness.

Largely because much social activity is dominated by private-sector production, the development of ideology in the typical developed capitalist society takes place both in the private sector (trade unions, churches, private universities) and within state institutions (public universities and schools, ministries of information). This leads many to believe that in the context of the bourgeois state, ideology can and does function relatively autonomously or independently of the repressive and executive arms of the state, much as the state itself can at times function autonomously or independently of the ruling class. The relative autonomy of ideology, however, like the autonomy of the state, masks—but does not obliterate—the essential class character of ideology in these societies. On the other hand, in the developed or peripheral capitalist societies that have fascist or authoritarian states and therefore a considerable state domination of production and labor—so that the spheres of social activity dominated by private-sector production are significantly narrowed—there is also usually a marked narrowing of the scope for the independent or autonomous development of ideology. This effect is of course amplified because state domination of the means of public communication is very obvious, as the propaganda machinery of Nazi Germany testifies. The result is that in such circumstances the ruling-class content of the dominant ideology becomes more obvious than in the typical bourgeois-democratic state.

Until fairly recently, the role of ideology has not been emphasized enough in the study of politics. The principal explanation for this situation in the Marxist literature has been the preoccupation with the "repressive" character of the capitalist state, interpeted here, as Poulantzas puts it, "in the strong sense of organized physical repression."[6] Poulantzas credits Miliband (in *The State in Capitalist Society*) with having restored the role of ideology to its rightful place in the analysis of the capitalist state. Poulantzas' main objective, however, was to develop the argument that there is a related tendency to confine the term ideology far too restrictively to ideas, customs, morals, and so on. As he put it:

> We have ended by considering that ideology only exists in ideas, customs, or morals without seeing that ideology can be embodied, in the strong sense, in *institutions:* institutions which

then, by the process of institutionalization, belong to the system of the state whilst depending critically on the ideological level.[7]

Poulantzas is claiming that ideology is often wrongly placed "outside" the state. He goes on to propose that:

> The system of the state is composed of several *apparatuses* or *institutions* of which certain have a repressive role, in the strong sense, and others a principally ideological role. The former constitutes the repressive apparatus of the state . . . the latter constitutes the *ideological apparatuses of the state*, such as the Church, the political parties, the unions (with the exception, of course, of the *revolutionary* party or trade union organization), the schools, the mass media (newspapers, radio, television) and, from a certain point of view, the family. This is so whether they are *public* or *private*—the distinction having a purely juridical, that is, largely ideological character.[8]

While acknowledging Gramsci's earlier insights, Poulantzas attributes a role to ideology that goes well beyond Gramsci and is close to the Althusserian formulation of "ideological state apparatuses," which include the following areas of social life: religion, education, the family, law, politics, trade unions, communications, culture—all of which are part of the instrumentalities of state domination in capitalist societies.[9]

As Miliband has observed, this formulation includes within the state a range of institutions that in bourgeois-democratic societies have been, and remain, part of "civil society."[10] To include them as part of the state is not only of theoretical concern—it contradicts previous Marxian analysis—but is of practical concern as well, because it affects the determination of the effective terrain of class struggle and of the political struggle for state power. The Poulantzas-Althusserian formulation errs in that it fails to acknowledge a vitally important disjuncture, which has been referred to many times above: the distinction between ruling-class power and state power. *Class power* (and with it class struggle over the power each class is to command) is reflected in the various institutions that are part of the ruling class's efforts to spread and maintain its hegemony over all areas of social life. But the power the ruling class has over society is much more general and much more all-encompassing than the power it derives from its ultimate control over the noneconomic force which is represented in the state. If, therefore, we equate state with society and treat all forms of class power as equal to state power, then by implication every area of social life must be seen as a manifestation of state power—and the state as an objectively existing institution disappears. This can be most clearly seen in the bourgeois-democratic state form, because there private-sector production is considerable and state domination of the means of communication is not fully developed. But it is also true—although less obvious—for fascist and authoritarian states, where the state seeks to assert all aspects of the ruling class's power, because even though private sector production is limited, the state can never be equal to the whole of society.

The general significance of the theoretical issues raised so far will be expanded upon in the next section, precisely because one of the major aspects of the development of the state in the periphery has been the rapid growth of its ideological function. As we noted in chapter 6, some writers (i.e., John Saul) have deemed this important enough to constitute the principal explanation for the unprecedented "centrality" of the state in peripheral capitalist formations.[11]

Ideology and the authoritarian state

In this section I shall examine certain aspects of the role of ideology in the authoritarian state. The first of these is that certain structural features of the periphery promote the rapid development of ideology, and also push it in a certain direction. Thus the highly fragmented and disarticulated production structures of these social formations, combined with their multiracial or multiethnic populations, encourage the vigorous promotion of the state as the principal unifying force and unifying symbol of the society. While it is recognized that racial and ethnic contradictions will affect the functioning of the state, ruling-class ideology presents the *state itself* as a symbol of unity among these contradictory forces.

Secondly, the underdevelopment of the main classes in these societies, which gives a leading and mediating role to the petty bourgeoisie and other intermediate strata, affects the direction that ideology develops in, as well as the rate at which this happens. For example, the state is frequently promoted as a stabilizing force that will counter the impermanence of the intermediate strata. Or again, the recentness of political independence has led to the promotion of the state as a unifying symbol, thus reinforcing its claims to exercise sovereignty on behalf of the community in the international sphere. In addition, poverty and economic backwardness, in conjunction with the rapid expansion of the "modernizing" and developmental functions of the state, encourages the promotion of the state as the symbol of unity amid diversity and poverty.

Third, the structural imperatives of these societies not only promote the role of ideology in social control, but also encourage certain key features of this ideology. For example, the state is invariably promoted as an institution "above and beyond class," representing in effect a simple equation of state and society. If this is taken as true, then the state is justified in treating criticism or attack as "subversive" and "antinational" activities. Furthermore, this ideology is very often accompanied by the line that leftist ideology preaches "hatred and war," as can be seen from the constant reference to "class struggle" and "class war." This becomes the ideological cover for a program of "eradication" of leftists—although in the political atmosphere that prevails as the authoritarian state develops, not only leftists but all those who contest the legitimacy of the regime become targets of physical repression. And as the church and humanitarian groups begin to protest the excesses of the state, the merest assertion of the elementary forms of democracy and human rights (whether they be free and fair elections, the right to organize in a trade union, or the right to freely publish and express dissenting opinions) makes them the object of state sanctions, up to and including execution by death squads.

Another key feature of the ideology of these states is the emphasis on the goals of development and modernization. Development is promoted as both an end in itself and as *the* principal objective of all social and economic activity. To be sure, such development is deliberately divorced from any consideration of social justice, equity, or democracy, and is instead measured in terms of new construction, the growth of the gross national product, the degree of literacy, and in some cases the extent to which the security forces carry modern equipment. Any attempt to challenge or defeat this conception of development is itself treated as "subversive" and "antinational," and thus is a legitimate reason for the exercise of state violence against its proponents.

This leads us to yet another feature of this ideology, which is the extent to which it is wrapped up in pseudo-socialist clothing. It is remarkable how many authoritarian states use pseudo-socialist rationalizations as the key planks of their manifestos.

As Paul Sweezy has observed, there is a

> grotesque caricature of utopian socialism in the form of a proliferation of pseudo-socialisms offered by all manner of politicians and parties to convince the masses that they stand for and will deliver a combination of the traditional ideals of socialism, together with what is supposed to be best in the familiar values of nationalism, religion, etc. Examples of this genre are "Arab Socialism," "African Socialism," "Indian Socialism," "Islamic Socialism"—every part of the Third World has its variant.[12]

Sweezy goes on to point to the reason for this:

> All these "socialisms" testify to the enormous appeal to the Third World's people of the original ideas of equality, cooperation, solidarity. At the same time, those who raise the banner of these particularistic "socialisms" . . . aim to gain and hold political power; and, given the conditions which have been inherited from the past, they can do this only by accepting and adapting to the center-periphery relationship of domination and subordination.[13]

One major result of seeking this type of legitimization is that "socialism," authoritarianism, and arbitrary rule have increasingly become equated in public consciousness, with the result that the struggle for "socialism" is divorced from the struggle to preserve and expand democratic political freedoms within the society. Indeed, as indicated in the previous chapter, the prevailing view is that political democracy and socialism stand in *opposition* to each other. The consequences of this confusion have been disastrous. First, it has weakened the defense of the masses in the immediate postcolonial period, when the flush of victory over colonialism was at its peak but the authoritarian state was already taking root. This helps to explain why it is not until the authoritarian state is fully constructed that there is a broad mass consciousness of what it represents.

The second effect of equating socialism and authoritarianism is that the entire project of creating a more equitable, socially just, and nonexploiting society is discredited. This perverse result clearly aids imperialism, not only because those on the "left" either accept (or reject as mere posturing) these states' self-description of themselves as socialist, but because the tendency in the imperialist camp has also been to promote the acceptance of this self-description, in the belief—apparently correct—that this will rebound to the disadvantage of the idea of socialism itself. It is this situation that in part led to the many gains of President Carter's short-lived "human rights" campaign, which sought to identify the virtues of equality, justice, fair play, etc., with the project of capitalism, and to identify the restriction of freedoms, arbitrary rule, etc., with the project of socialism. Those authoritarian states that propound a leftist ideology therefore offer the working masses the worst of both worlds—neither socialism nor a reasonable pretense to bourgeois-democratic forms of rule.

The final feature of ruling-class ideology is its effort to ensure that its pronouncements are confined to generalities. Phrases such as "law and order," the "necessities of development," and so on, never are translated into *whose* law, *whose* order, development for *whom*, and then answered in concrete terms. On the contrary, since the effort is to conceal the real relations of production, class divisions, and the exploitation inherent in the methods of surplus extraction and appropriation, there is great resistance to any attempt to articulate and coherently develop (that is, systematize) the world views represented by these ideas. This contrasts strongly with practice in the center countries where, because of the longer and more deeply rooted intellectual tradition, the greater development of universities, journals of analysis and opinion, and so on, the systematization of the democratic (or even imperialist) world view is well developed, even among the major political parties. In peripheral capitalist societies, on the other hand, there is little pretense at logic and/or presenting an internally consistent view. Since the populace is believed to be undereducated, reliance is placed on the manipulation of public opinion by exploiting the technical and psychological resources of modern mass communication. Thus is the local ruling class's contempt for the broad mass of population in the periphery dramatically revealed.

Long ago Marx pointed out the eventual effect that this would have on the ruling class and on the population at large:

> The government hears only *its own voice*, and yet hangs on the illusions that it hears the voice of the people; and it demands that the people likewise hang on to this illusion. On its part, therefore, the people sink partly into political superstition, partly into political skepticism, or withdrawn from political life, they become a *privatized rabble*.[14]

The degeneration of political activity that accompanies the rise of the authoritarian state must be placed in the wider context of the degeneration of culture that also accompanies the dissemination of ruling-class ideology in peripheral capitalist societies. When culture and national consciousness are constantly manipulated in order to support the prevailing system of domination and exploitation, the potential for liberation—which seemed to exist during the struggle against colonial oppression—may no longer appear to do so. This is what Frantz Fanon referred to as the "pitfalls of national consciousness"[15]—not so subtle and continuous attempts are made by the ruling class to divide and rule by manipulating the awareness of ethnic, tribal, or racial divisions. Ironically, this occurs at the same time that the state is being proclaimed as the symbol of unity of all the people!

Whatever the situation when colonial power was transferred to the local state, increased repression is the dialectical accompaniment of the decreasing popularity of the regime in power. This repression is invariably combined with an effort to promote a charismatic leader, in the belief that such a leader will symbolize the unity of the whole people, will stand above class—and even above the government and state machinery—and that this will create a large political space within which the ruling class can maneuver. However, one characteristic that distinguishes the authoritarian state from its fascist counterpart is the failure to develop and sustain a mass party or mass movement of the necessary dimensions. Even where the ruling party may once have had significant political support, the intensification of class contradictions, splits arising from intraclass rivalries (usually expressed in competition between two potential political leaders), the growing repression of popular expression, and the immiserizing consequences of the structural economic crisis invariably produce a considerable loss of political support. It is at this point that the electoral system is seized and free and fair elections are no longer possible. To compensate for the declining appeal of the ruling party, state functionaries operate in place of party activists and public support is generated by forcing crowds to gather under the penalty of victimization. That is why the crowds that come to acclaim the leader are made up of state employees, members of the disciplined services, students at state schools, and members of pliant unions—all coerced in one way or another to attend. These manifestations of the "popularity" of the authoritarian state play an important role in the ruling class's manipulation of mass consciousness. The result has generally been, however, that on the day such governments are overthrown, the very crowds that were forced to applaud them turn out to applaud their demise!

In marked contrast to the European fascist states, the role of so-called ideological nationalism—the racist ideology of the fascist parties—is not particularly developed in the authoritarian state.[16] Three factors account for this. One is that the ruling groups in these latter countries are much more "open" and "dependent," because of their role in the overall system of imperialist domination, than in their fascist counterparts; and while the dominant imperialist classes may overlook dictatorial state forms and support the persecution and elimination of "communists," they usually draw the line at fascist ideological nationalism, which they fear may lead to the irrational disruption of imperialist relations and indirectly affect their own societies. Second, colonial rule itself has had a fairly dampening effect on traditional and other national ties in the ideology of the ruling strata in the periphery—colonial rule required the oppression of the culture of *all* the groups in the colonial territory. Third, the general worldwide improvement in education and communication has modified the ability of groups to promote this type of racist ideology openly (although whether this will remain true is in doubt).

The international character of ideological domination

The way in which the peripheral capitalist formations are inserted into the capitalist world system ensures that the authoritarian state is a part of the international structure of imperialist domination. As noted before, the authoritarian state develops not only in response to internal contradictions within the peripheral capitalist formations, but also in response to contradictions that derive from the place these societies hold within the imperialist system. Insofar, therefore, as ruling-class ideology serves the same objective as does the state—that of maintaining ruling-class domination—the role of ideology and its relation to the state must be viewed within the worldwide hierarchical system of domination. There is, in other words, an international system of domination and both the locally dominant economic interests and those that control the state are part of it.

The truth of this is obvious if we examine the control over the means of communication and information that is exercised by the center countries. Transnational corporations based in these countries control the major news agencies, data banks and information retrieval systems, the publishing houses, magazines, and the production and dissemination of radio and television programs, films, documentaries, and so on. The result is a continuous flow of ideology at the international level that supports the existing international order. Indeed, this onesided flow has been so extreme as to be counterproductive, since it has provoked resistance in many peripheral societies. This resistance—which is part of a wider cultural assertiveness in the periphery—has found expression in the class for a new international information and communications order, a counterpart to the new international economic order. Unfortunately, this is not as progressive and anti-imperialist a development as it might seem, since previous experience has shown that the governments behind it see a new international information and communication order as the means of ensuring their *own* control of these media, and thus of increasing their ability to support their domination.

It is one of the many mystifications of capitalist ideology that in the name of "security," "freedom," "defense against Communist subversion," and so on, there has been a stream of ideology from the center to the periphery that is aimed at reinforcing the most nonparticipatory, authoritarian structures and outlook in the latter. Despite occasional exposés of terrorist rule and undemocratic practice, the information and communications media in the center countries have generally sought to promote the legitimacy of such regimes—the only condition being that they do not espouse causes that directly conflict with the interests of imperialism. As a result, if such regimes take an openly pro-Western, pro-private enterprise, and otherwise "rightist" stance, a great effort is made by the governments in the center countries to ensure their "respectability" in the international community. (This does not mean, however, that the ruling classes in the center favor despotic, fascistic, or other dictatorial forms of the state for themselves.)

The existence of an international structure of ideological domination, with the center countries (and in particular the United States) at its apex, does not necessarily result in a crude uniformity in the propagation of capitalist ideology. On the contrary, since the objective task of this international structure is to support the development of capitalism, it can only do so effectively if it adapts to the correct configurations of capitalist development. Such configurations not only flow along the lines of the center-periphery distinction but also reflect cultural, regional, and local peculiarities within these broad groupings. To take an example, it is obvious that the open and rabid anti-communism and anti-socialism of the U.S. version of capitalist ideology does not sit well in such capitalist countries as France and Italy, where Communist parties are sufficiently well entrenched to have participated in governments (or to expect to do so). Similarly, capitalist ideology cannot be effectively propagandized in the Islamic world if it is separated from the Islamic underpinnings of the society. This adaptability is an essential component of the international structure of ideology, and creates the "appearance" of pragmatism in the capitalist analysis of the present world order.

Finally, just as the different ideologies of center and periphery reflect real social differences, so the ideologies in the periphery itself will differ as they are adapted to differing conditions.

9. Conclusion: Oppression and Liberation

My analysis would not be complete without an examination of its implications for political struggle. After all, the true function of social analysis is not scholastic understanding for its own sake; it is to enrich our social practice. The exceptionally dominating, brutal, and terroristic character of the recent postcolonial state underscores the significance of this observation. Just as European fascism was not "a mere passing episode in the automatic process of growing economic crisis–evolution–catastrophe–revolution [which was] somehow supposed to crumble of its own accord,"[1] so too the authoritarian state cannot be expected to crumble of *its* own accord. On the contrary, it will require the bitterest of political struggles to smash this state and commence the process of liberation and socialist construction in the periphery.

Before outlining the political practice that follows directly from the analysis in this book, a brief recapitulation of a few significant features of the authoritarian state is necessary. The first of these is that the authoritarian state does not mark the end of a process of political degeneration and crisis in recent postcolonial societies. Further stages of reaction are possible, including military dictatorship and the accompanying repression of all surviving quasilegal independent organizations. Second, the authoritarian state—or its further degeneration—develops out of a crisis and must be understood as the ruling class's response to a popular offensive that has been gaining ground. Thus the repression that presently characterizes the southern cone of South America (Chile, Brazil, Uruguay), South Korea, Guyana, and the Phillipines, or the repression of Idi Amin's Uganda, the Shah's Iran, or Eric Gairy's Grenada proceeds directly from the intense anticapitalist, anti-imperialist, and domestic struggles waged in these countries. Similarly, the present mass offensive in many parts of Central America and the Caribbean may lead to repression on a similar scale if the popular forces do not succeed in seizing—and, most important of all, holding—state power.[2]

Third, although I believe that the authoritarian state is the most likely development in the present conjuncture, there is nothing automatic about its rise. I have been careful to stress that the authoritarian state is only *one of several possible ruling-class responses* to the crisis facing recent postcolonial societies. It is therefore not an inevitable stage of development in postcolonial societies, or in the periphery in general; nor does it possess any other universal or "automatic" characteristics.

Fourth, since the state in the periphery must perform the role of capitalist and lead in the process of capital accumulation, it has a unique potential for shaping society. This is obvious in the role the state plays in the formation of classes, particularly its role in securing an economic base for the expanded reproduction of the ruling class.

Fifth, although the authoritarian state is an exceptional state, and not an ordinarily succeeding state, there are *limits to its capacity*, just as there are limits to the capacity of the capitalist state. These limits are set by the location of these states in the system of economic reproduction and by the form that accumulation takes.

Finally, since the authoritarian state emerges in the context of imperialism, political strategies to deal with it must explicitly take into account this aspect of its international structure.

Oppression and liberation are dialectically related, and it has been important to specify the form of the state correctly in order to combine correct theory with practice. In light of this, what is correct political practice in these circumstances?

The first and perhaps most important conclusion is that since the authoritarian state exercises a special form of class domination—it removes the possibility of an ordinary legal or constitutional succession of governments—it cannot be defeated without a democratic alliance of *all* the major classes, strata, and social groups and their organizations (whether they be political, economic, or social) that are directly affected by this system of state domination. This strategy is similar to the "united front" proposals that emerged in the 1930s in order to confront fascism in Europe. However, although it is identical in principle, when it is applied to the periphery a different range and variety of organizations are affected. Further, efforts to form such an alliance should not be approached in purely tactical or strategic terms, as was the case with the "united front" in Europe. Since the authoritarian state develops in peripheral capitalist societies that have *not* gone through a "bourgeois-democratic" transformation of political and state relations, the alliance is necessary to combat this state, for without a democratic transformation there can be no real movement toward socialist transformation. The task of the alliance therefore goes further than bringing about a change of government, with the state structure remaining more or less intact and with a "bourgeois-democratic" path resumed. What is at stake is a fundamental transformation of state and political relations in favor of the popular forces, in a situation where this has never been the case before. This is a minimum achievement, and without it there is considerable doubt as to whether the society can proceed beyond its present stage of social development. If the objective of the alliance is other than this, then the solution will be a coup, military or otherwise; as we all know, this occurs frequently in these societies—and just as frequently yields no changes of substance.

Since the alliance is a matter of fundamental principle, the bottom line for the involvement of various social categories in the struggle is determined by their commitment to democratic political practice. In this approach there is no room for the dogmatic and purist view of alliances adhered to by some Marxist parties and groups. This caution is important, since in the Marxist political tradition there is deep distrust of so-called cross-class alliances. While I will return to this issue shortly, here I want to make the point that in approaching the issue of alliances, naive judgements should not be made about the capacity of bourgeois forces in these societies, despite the underdevelopment of the bourgeoisie. Equally, however, socialist forces cannot afford to make concessions that will restrict the independent organization of the working class, since it is precisely this restriction that has favored the growth of the authoritarian state and has stalled the project of socialist transformation.

The experiences of Latin America, both during the period of the guerrilla *focos* and during the present period of "peoples' war" (the latter broadly defined to include the present Central American experiences), show that the strategy of making alliances in the struggle for state power must be informed by a deep appreciation of the complex forms of struggle that must be pursued, and in particular must gauge the correct emphasis on guerrilla/military actions. While the authoritarian state is distinguished by its prevention of any legal or constitutional means of changing governments, Marxists cannot be indifferent to the degrees of legality that exist in these societies. Guerrilla actions, taken in isolation from other segments of the popular forces (trade unions, churches, democratic political parties, professional associations, etc.) are just as futile as political actions that do not recognize that the authoritarian state will neither crumble nor lose its grip on the society of its own accord.

In many recent postcolonial societies there are a variety of ethnic, social, and regional groups. This means that the effort to build alliances of popular and democratic forces must be based on an appreciation of racial, sexual, and other forms of oppression. This is necessary if all oppressed groups are to be brought into the alliance. A similar sensitivity must be displayed when dealing with other popular ideological currents, such as liberation theology. In other words, the watchword is *unity*—unity inspired by the fact that the authoritarian state is not the result of an ordinary succession of states. And because of the highly fluid and complex social structures of the periphery, such unity requires great skill and commitment to democratic practice in order to survive.

This leads directly to a second major proposition, which is that where the authoritarian state has consolidated itself, *it is necessary for the society to pass through a democratic phase of political struggle*. The success of the popular forces during this stage not only makes possible the democratic transformation of political and state relations, but creates also the sociopolitical base for a complementary relationship between the struggles for socialism and the struggles for political democracy. Ultimately, the authoritarian state has survived because of its capacity to exclude the working class and peasantry from political power, and acknowledging the necessity of a democratic phase of struggle requires that the leading political forces realize that the establishment of a sociopolitical basis for the independent organization of the working class and peasantry is necessary before any serious socialist advance can be contemplated.

The question that arises is how long such a democratic stage will last. The answer is that whether it is a few months, a few years, or a few decades cannot be determined *a priori*. Only the concrete conditions of each society and the quality of political leadership displayed by the popular forces can provide the answers. However, the dangers of failing to recognize the objective nature of this phase of social struggle in the periphery are well known. These range from misjudged attempts at "forced collectivism" and the "elimination of dissidents" to premature engagements with imperialism based on a self-promoted identification with the socialist/Soviet bloc.

The democratic phase of popular struggle, with its emphasis on mobilizing democratic forces to remove the regime in power and to ensure the establishment of democratic and representative institutions, the legalization of political parties and trade unions, and so on, has a significance at the economic as well as political and ideological levels. This should be obvious, since the independent organization of the workers and peasants cannot take place in the absence of a secure economic base for the reproduction and progressive enhancement of the role of these classes in the system of economic production. This has implications for the forms of property ownership, the patterns of accumulation and resource use, commercial relations with other states, the system of wage determination and collective bargaining, and the forms of organization of rural society. Again, it is not possible to determine *a priori* the economic strategy that should be pursued—this must emerge from the concrete circumstances—but it is clear that within the objective constraints posed by the stage of development, progressive efforts have to be made to democratize the economy by altering many of its colonial and neocolonial aspects—the growth of democratic and independent trade unions must be facilitated, worker control in state enterprises provided, accountable agencies to manage public bodies created, peasant organizations legalized and protected, and so on. In order to minimize subsequent disagreements, the broad contours of an economic program should be negotiated at the beginning of the alliance.

The construction of a broad alliance along the lines indicated here raises the issue of the relations of left parties to other democratic parties. It is taken for granted that the pivotal factor in the long-run transformation of peripheral capitalism is the construction of a worker-peasant alliance capable of winning and wielding power through its democratic organizations. Because of this, the cornerstone of the alliance must be an alliance of left parties. This is, unfortunately, much easier said than done. The problem most frequently encountered is that many left parties do not share the political strategy outlined here, and favor a vanguard approach, with a political-military offensive waged by the left parties alone. In this view, other parties are only "permitted" to participate on conditions laid down by the left parties in the alliance. It is clear that this position prevents broad unity; those left parties that support the political line proposed here may then form alliances with other political parties. The question of how to proceed in this situation cannot be answered without considering the concrete realities of each society, but the danger is that the left forces will split, which will only weaken the mass movement.

Because specifying the state form correctly is absolutely essential if a correct political strategy is to be determined, the problem of diagnosing the state form arises. The problem is how to discern an authoritarian state in its early stages. The quasilegal status of political parties during the early period of development, the combination of open terror with a facade of parliamentarianism/constitutionality, the manipulation of the media and mass consciousness, the administrative/police methods of restraining freedom, and the ability to discriminate economically against all sections of the population all serve to make this diagnosis very difficult indeed. Furthermore, after the diagnosis is made there is the added difficulty of convincing the masses, other democratic strata and groups, and so on, of the irreversibility of this tendency. What often happens is that the reality is not admitted until open terror, political murder, and the militarization of the society are so blatant that no one can be deceived any longer. Thus it is often not until these states are fully entrenched and all overt political work is highly dangerous—if not prohibited—that the need to build an alliance of democratic forces is widely accepted. At this stage, however, the alliance must be fought for in a situation where almost all the political parties/organizations are either in exile or are surviving in some form of underground existence. To achieve unity at this stage is very difficult, particularly when there is no experience of working together politically inside the country to draw upon. Nevertheless, the period between diagnosis by the vanguard elements of the political leadership and the masses' acceptance of the reality is one that can be used creatively, to get long-term advantage.

Needless to say, the struggle against the authoritarian state is the struggle against imperialism. The strategy of internal alliances must therefore have an external component. Since, however, the internal alliance is governed by the objective requirements of a democratic phase of the struggle to build socialism, the external component must also reflect this reality. This means that a major objective must be to win the support of the "socialist" bloc, the progressive wing of the nonaligned movement, and social-democratic forces within the capitalist center countries. This is possible—if extremely difficult—because of the democratic character of the political struggle, and the composition of the alliance, within these countries. Failure to appreciate this has led to the outright rejection of the support of democratic forces in the center countries, or to political opportunism in accepting it. The success of the Vietnamese struggle in winning the support of a broad range of democratic groups in Europe and the United States (students, social-democratic parties, etc.) ought to have made this lesson very obvious, but it was not until the Nicaraguans began to apply it that it became better appreciated on the left—though much skepticism remains.

This international strategy cannot be undertaken with disregard for such other objective circumstances as the size of the country; its regional, hemispheric, and global strategic importance; the history of its border relations with other states; and its monopoly status in world commodity markets. As these vary from country to country, general prescriptions are impossible, but priority must *always* be given to mobilizing support in the region where the particular country is located. Such a strategy can draw upon cultural, historical, and even nationalist sentiments. It is not infrequent for those who oppress human rights in their own countries to champion the struggle against such oppression in a neighboring country, once these struggles have reached a certain stage of public debate and support. In any case, the need to neutralize these territories so that they do not become bases for imperialist intervention is great enough to ensure great attention to the regional context.

The struggle for broad-based international support also serves to bolster the internal development of a mass movement that will confront the ruling regime. To this extent, therefore, it reduces the temptation to opt for putchist-type solutions, which may succeed in ousting the government but will not succeed in fundamentally transforming political and state relations.

In conclusion, it is freely admitted that the greatest danger in the strategy proposed here is that it will degenerate into a "social-democratic" path. While some may consider such a development far better than the perpetuation of the authoritarian state–military dictatorship syndrome, it is also far short of a genuine movement in the direction of socialist transformation. This risk exists, and must be confronted; and, based on Marxist historical materialist analysis, a practice must be devised to head it off. I have no patience with those who argue that a "left" authoritarian state is preferable to a social-democratic one; both are degenerations in the struggle for socialism. In the context of peripheral capitalism, the particular danger of the former is that it can delay the movement to political democratic forms, which constitute the minimum necessary for the social advance of the workers and peasantry in the periphery.

Once again, therefore, oppression and liberation are indeed dialectically related, and the strategy developed in the fight for liberation must be guided by the nature of the oppression of the vast majority of the population. The source of that oppression is not, and never has been, located in the composition of the existing government; it is rooted in the structure of social relations, classes, and the organization and levels of development of the productive forces. The struggle to overcome this must therefore be guided by a larger vision or the left will be guilty of the same historical shortsightedness with which the present ruling classes exercise state power, a shortsightedness that is revealed in their gratuitous brutality, the daily affronts they heap on our concepts of self- and human worth, and in the thinly disguised contempt for the masses of the population in whose name they claim the "right" to rule.

Notes

Introduction

1. Nicos Poulantzas, "The Problem of the Capitalist State," *New Left Review* 58 (November-December 1969): 68.
2. N. Bobbio, "Is There a Marxist Theory of the State?" *Telos* (Spring 1978): 5–16.
3. Ibid., p. 5.
4. H. Goulbourne, *Politics and State in the Third World* (London, 1979), p. ix. It might be added in all fairness that the Latin American literature on the state and politics in these societies has greatly exceeded in quantity and quality that emanating from the English-speaking parts of the Third World.
5. See, as representative of these schools: J. Holloway and S. Ricciotto, eds., *State and Capital: A Marxist Debate* (London, 1978); E. Altvater, "Notes on Some Problems of State Interventionism," *Kapitalistate* 1 (1973): 96–108; Ernesto Laclau, "The Specificity of the Political: Around the Poulantzas-Miliband Debate," *Economy and Society* 5, no. 1 (1975): 87-110; D. Gold, C. H. Lo, and E. O. Wright, "Recent Developments in Marxist Theories of the Capitalist State," *Monthly Review* 27, no. 5 (1975): 29–43; Nicos Poulantzas, *Political Power and Social Classes* (London, 1973), *Fascism and Dictatorship* (London, 1974), *The Crisis of Dictatorship* (London, 1976); and Ralph Miliband, *The State in Capitalist Society* (London, 1969), and *Marxism and Politics* (London, 1977).
6. Hal Draper, *Karl Marx's Theory of Revolution*, Part I, Books I and II (New York, 1977).
7. See Hamza Alava, "The State in Post-Colonial Societies: Pakistan and Bangladesh," *New Left Review*, no. 75 (July–August 1972): 59–81; Colin Leys, "The 'Overdeveloped' Post-Colonial State: A Re-Evaluation," *Review of Radical Political Economy* (January–April 1976): 39–48; John S. Saul, "The State in Post-Colonial Societies: Tanzania," *Socialist Register 1974* (London, 1974), pp. 249–72; Issa Shivji, *Class Struggle in Tanzania* (New York and London, 1976); Mahmoud Mamdami, *Politics and Class Formation in Uganda* (New York and London, 1976).
8. See W. Ziemann and M. Lanzendörfer, "The State in Peripheral Societies," *Socialist Register 1977* (London, 1977), pp. 143–47;

W. Heim and K. Stenzel, "The Capitalist State and Underdevelopment in Latin America," *Kapitalistate* 2 (1973): 31–48.

9. As examples see James Petras, *Critical Perspectives on Imperialism and Social Class in the Third World* (New York and London, 1982); A. Cueva, "The Latin American State in the Crisis of Capitalism," *Second Congress of Third World Economists* (Havana, 1981); "Fascismo y economía en América Latina," *Controversia* (Mexico) 1, no. 2 (1977): 37–43. L. Hammergran, "Corporatism in Latin American Politics," *Comparative Politics* 9, no. 4 (1977): 443–61; F. Mires, "Para una critica de la teoria del fascismo Latinoamericano," *Nueva Sociedad* (November/December 1979): 22–45; E. Myllmaki, "The Problem of Militarism in Latin America," *Ibero-Americano* (Stockholm) 7, no. 2 (1978): 68–76; J. Malloy, ed., *Authoritarianism in Latin America* (Pittsburgh, 1977); A. Boron, "New Forms of Capitalist State in Latin America: An Exploration," *Race and Class* 20, no. 3 (Winter 1979): 263–76; F. H. Cardoso and E. Faletto, "Estado y proceso politico en America Latina," *Rev. Mexicana de Sociologia* (April/June 1977); D. Collier, ed., *The New Authoritarianism in Latin America* (Princeton, N.J., 1979); G. O'Donnell, *Modernization and Bureaucratic Authoritarianism: Studies in South American Politics* (Berkeley, Ca., 1973); A. Stephap, ed., *Authoritarian Brazil: Origins, Politics, and Future* (New Haven, 1973); J. J. Linz, "Totalitarian and Authoritarian Regimes," *Handbook of Political Science*, ed. F. Greenstein and N. Polsby (Reading, Mass., 1975).

10. N. Bobbio, "Is There a Marxist Theory of the State?" *Telos* (Spring 1978): 8.

11. Miliband, *Marxism and Politics*, p. 83.

12. Ibid., p. 82.

13. Clive Y. Thomas, "The Non-Capitalist Path as Theory and Practice of Decolonization and Socialist Transformation," *Latin American Perspectives* 5, no. 2 (Spring 1978): 10–28; reprinted in A. Y. Yansane, ed., *Decolonization and Dependency* (London, 1980), pp. 231–51.

1: Colonialism, Slavery, and the Emergence of the State

1. Hal Draper, *Karl Marx's Theory of Revolution*, vol. 1 (New York, 1977), p. 243.

2. The following pages draw from my study, *Plantations, Peasants, and the State: A Study of the Modes of Sugar Production in Guyana* (Los Angeles and Kingston, Jamaica, 1983). See also A. K. Adamson, *Sugar Without Slaves* (New Haven, 1972).

3. See Lloyd Best, "A Model of Pure Plantation Economy," *Social and Economic Studies* (September 1968).
4. See J. Banaji, "For a Theory of Colonial Modes of Production," *Economic and Political Weekly* 23 (December 1972): 249.

2: Transition: The Emergence of Labor

1. See Harry Magdoff, *Imperialism: From the Colonial Age to the Present* (New York, 1978), pp. 17–75.
2. An excellent work that develops on the theme of colonialism as a materialist category is C. A. Green, "Towards a Theory of 'Colonial' Modes of Production: A Marxist Approach," M.A. thesis, University of Toronto, 1980.

3: The Emergence of Peripheral Capitalism

1. E. R. Davson, *British Guiana and Its Development*, quoted in H. A. Lutchman, *From Colonialism to Cooperative Republic* (Puerto Rico, 1974), p. 187.
2. As an example, the Constitution was suspended in Guyana in 1928 (and again in 1953) when elections led to popular elements critical of colonial interests dominating the elective positions.

5: Class Structure and the State in the Periphery

1. On localization see Clive Y. Thomas, *Dependence and Transformation: The Economics of the Transition to Socialism* (New York, 1974), pp. 87–98, and "Meaningful Participation: The Fraud of It," in David Lowenthal and Lambros Comitas, eds., *The Aftermath of Sovereignty* (New York, 1973).
2. See Clive Y. Thomas, "Socialist-Capitalist Economic Relations and the Struggle for a New International Economic Order," *Transition* 2, no. 1 (1979).
3. See Carl Stone, "Decolonization and the Caribbean State System: The Case of Jamaica," in *The Newer Caribbean: Decolonization, Democracy, and Development*, ed. Paget Henry and Carl Stone (Philadelphia, 1983), pp. 41–42.

4. Thomas, *Dependence and Transformation*, p. 87.
5. See Issa Shivji, *Class Struggles in Tanzania* (New York and London, 1976), in particular chart 2 on p. 88.

6: State Power and Class Power

1. See Hamza Alavi, "The State in Post-Colonial Societies: Pakistan and Bangladesh," *New Left Review* 74 (July–August 1972): 59–82.
2. S. Girling, "The State in Post-Colonial Societies—Pakistan and Bangladesh," comments on M. Alavi's article, *Kapitalstate* 2 (1973): 49–51.
3. Alavi, "The State in Post-Colonial Societies," p. 61.
4. See in particular Colin Leys, "The 'Overdeveloped' Post-Colonial State: A Re-evaluation," *Review of African Political Economy* 5 (January–April 1976): 39–48; and W. Ziemann and M. Lanzendörfer, "The State in Peripheral Societies," *Socialist Register 1977* (London, 1977), pp. 143–77.
5. Leys, "The 'Overdeveloped' Post-Colonial State," p. 42.
6. Ziemann and Lanzendörfer, "The State in Peripheral Societies," p. 145.
7. See John Saul, "The State in Post-Colonial Societies: Tanzania," *Socialist Register 1974* (London, 1974), pp. 349–72.
8. In addition to the points listed in the text, Articles 21(a) and (b) of the constitution of the ruling party read as follows:

   If the leader in his deliberate judgement is of the opinion that a situation of emergency has arisen in the party, he shall have power, notwithstanding any provision in these rules, on giving written notice to the General Secretary of his opinion, to take all action that he may in his absolute discretion consider necessary to correct such a situation; and for this purpose he may assume and exercise any or all of the powers of the Biennial Delegates Conference, the General Council, the Central Executive Committee, any other committee, arm, organ, or of any officer or official of the party. If the General Council, the Central Executive Committee or the Administration Committee has not been constituted or for any reason cannot function, the Leader may exercise all or any of its power or may authorise such members as he may deem fit to exercise its powers for the time being.

   In the recently promulgated national constitution of Guyana, the president is head of state, supreme executive authority, and commander-in-chief. He is also head of the national assembly, the local democratic organs, the national congress of local democratic organs, and the supreme congress of the people—all state organs created under the constitution. This supremacy is given through his power "to summon, suspend, or dissolve" all of these "democratic" and "supreme" organs, and through his veto power over the national assembly. In addition, the president appoints the chairman of the elections commission, the chairman of the public service commission, the chairman of the police service commission, and has the right to appoint either a majority of the members, or in some cases all the members, of these commissions. In addition, he appoints the army chief of staff, all army commanders, the director-general of the national service and all of his deputies, the commissioner of police and all of his deputies, the attorney general, the chancellor of the judiciary, the chief justice, the director of public prosecution, and literally every other important official in the state. The constitution further states (Article 182 (1)) that the president

> shall not be personally answerable to any court for the performance of the functions of his office or for any act done in the performance of those functions, and no proceedings, whether criminal or civil, shall be instituted against him in his personal capacity in respect thereof either during his term of office or thereafter.

This example should make clear the extreme degrees to which executive domination of the state can be taken under the guise of "constitutionality" in the periphery!

9. Hal Draper, *Karl Marx's Theory of Revolution*, Part I: *State and Bureaucracy* (New York, 1977), p. 321.
10. Ibid., pp. 321–22; emphasis in original.
11. Ibid., p. 322.
12. Ibid., p. 323.
13. On this, see Ziemann and Lazendörfer, "The State in Peripheral Societies."
14. F. Engels, letter to C. Schmidt, October 27, 1980, in Karl Marx and Friedrich Engels, *Selected Correspondence* (Moscow, 1960), p. 504.
15. Ralph Miliband, *Marxism and Politics* (London, 1977), pp. 87–88.

7: The Rise of the Authoritarian State

1. For data on militarization in Guyana, see G. K. Danns, "Militarization and Development: An Experiment in Nation Building," *Transition* 1, no. 1 (1978): 23–44. In this article Danns points out that 1 in every 35 persons in Guyana belongs to one or other security service. This estimate does not include the "unknown" bodies of men armed by the state, and the private armed bodies attached to leading members of the ruling political party.
2. E. Ahmad, "The Neo-Fascist State: Notes on the Pathology of

Power in the Third World," *International Foundation for Development Alternatives* (September/October, 1980): 2(16).

3. Ibid.: 3(17).
4. Ibid.
5. Ibid.
6. Ibid.
7. Noam Chomsky and Edward Herman, *The Washington Connection and Third World Fascism* (Boston, 1979), p. 44.
8. See Michael Klare, *Supplying Repression: U.S. Support for Authoritarian Regimes Abroad* (Washington, D.C., 1977).
9. See H. Goulbourne, ed., *Politics and the State in the Third World* (London, 1979), p. 119.
10. See my " 'The Non-Capitalist Path' as Theory and Practice of Decolonization and Socialist Transformation," *Latin American Perspectives* (Spring 1978): 10–28.
11. Quoted in Rosa Luxemburg, *Selected Political Writings*, R. Looker, ed. (New York, 1974), pp. 244–47.
12. N. Bobbio, "Are There Alternatives to Representative Democracy?" *Telos* 35 (Spring 1978): 30.
13. Nicos Poulantzas, "Towards a Democratic Socialism," *New Left Review* 109 (June 1978): 80.
14. Ibid., p. 87.
15. Ibid.
16. See A. Boron, "New Forms of Capitalist State in Latin America: An Exploration," *Race and Class* 20, no. 3 (Winter 1979): 263–64. In Italy and Germany the counter-revolution acquired the unique and distinctive traits of the fascist state. In other countries the authoritarian response gave place to regressive Bonapartist regimes (in Gramsci's conceptualization) or, simply, to the rise of military dictatorships which, using a variety of methods, put an end to political crises and curbed the revolutionary offensive of the popular masses.
17. For references, see note 9 of the introduction.
18. David Collier, ed., *The New Authoritarianism in Latin America*, p. 4.
19. G. O'Donnell, "Tensions in the Bureaucratic-Authoritarian State and the Question of Democracy," in ibid., p. 292.
20. Ibid.
21. To be sure, queries have been raised about the accuracy of the claim that the import-substitution model is exhausted. A. O. Hirschman, for example, has questioned whether such an exhaustion can occur or whether there are not cycles of import substitution at the end of which new stimuli are needed for it to re-emerge. Because of such queries, many compare the experiences of Argentina (1966–1970 and post-1976), Chile (post-1973), and Brazil (post-1964), with Colombia, Venezuela, and Mexico in order to prove that the exhaustion of this process of industrialization is not

the cause of the emergence of the bureaucratic-authoritarian state. In my approach not only is the crisis highly generalized but there is also no rigid, determinist, linear explanation linking the exhaustion of the import-substitution model to the rise of the authoritarian state. The emergence of this state forms "one option" but not the only option facing the ruling classes. See A. O. Hirschman, "The Turn to Authoritarianism in Latin America and the Search for Its Economic Determinants," in ibid., pp. 61–98.

8: Ideology and the Authoritarian State

1. K. Marx and F. Engels, The German Ideology (New York, 1970), pp. 65–66.
2. Ibid., p. 64.
3. John McMurty, The Structure of Marx's World-View (Princeton, N.J., 1978), p. 141.
4. There is of course a major philosophical issue here. One view that I do not want to recapitulate here but that has influenced my understanding of this complex problem is that of John McMurty in ibid.
5. Karl Marx, Capital, Vol. I (New York, 1967), p. 72.
6. Nicos Poulantzas, "The Problem of the Capitalist State," in Robin Blackburn, ed., Ideology in Social Science (New York, 1973), p. 250.
7. Ibid., pp. 250–51; emphasis in the original.
8. Ibid., p. 251; emphasis in the original.
9. Louis Althusser, "Ideology and Ideological State Apparatuses (Notes Towards an Investigation)," in Lenin and Philosophy (New York and London, 1971), p. 143.
10. Ralph Miliband, Marxism and Politics (London, 1977), pp. 54–57.
11. John Saul, "The State in Post-Colonial Societies: Tanzania," in Socialist Register 1974 (London, 1974), p. 349.
12. P. Sweezy, "Socialism in Poor Countries," Monthly Review 28, no. 5 (October 1976): 7–8.
13. Ibid., p. 8.
14. Karl Marx, "Debates on Freedom of the Press," in Karl Marx and Friederich Engels, Werke, 1: 63–64 as quoted in H. Draper, Karl Marx's Theory of Revolution, vol. 1 (New York and London: Monthly Review Press, 1977), p. 49.
15. Frantz Fanon, The Wretched of the Earth (New York, 1965).
16. This is not to deny the existence of racist appeals, or such elements of Nazi ideology as the promotion of the Jewish stereotype, as in Argentina.

9: Conclusion

1. N. Poulantzas, *Fascism and Dictatorship* (London: New Left Books, 1974), p. 48.
2. We stress the *holding of power*, since the example of Chile indicates that if power is recaptured from left forces a program of extermination and other such brutalities against the left is immediately set in motion. The ruling class in fact reacts more violently at having lost and then regained power than at as yet unsuccessful assaults on its power.

Selected Reading

Adamson, A. H. *Sugar Without Slaves: The Political Economy of British Guiana, 1838–1904*. New Haven and London, 1972.

Ahmad, E. "The Neo-Fascist State: Notes on the Pathology of Power in the Third World." *International Foundation for Development Alternatives* 19 (September–October 1980): 15–26.

Alavi, H. "The State in Post-Colonial Societies: Pakistan and Bangladesh." *New Left Review* 74 (July–August 1972): 59–81.

Altvater, E. "Notes on Some Problems of State Interventionism." *Kapitalstate* 1 (1973): 96–108.

———— et al. "On the Analysis of Imperialism in the Metropolitan Countries: The West German Example." *Bulletin of the Conference of Socialist Economists* (Spring 1974): 1–24.

————. "Some Problems of State Interventionism." In *State and Capital*, edited by J. Holloway and S. Picciotto. London, 1978.

Ambursley, F. and Cohen, R. *Crisis in the Caribbean*. New York and London, 1984.

Amin, S. *Class and Nation, Historically and in the Current Crisis*. New York and London, 1980.

Arismendi, R. "Fascism and Its Manifestations in Latin America." *Tricontinental* (Havana) 64 (1979).

Banaji, J. "For a Theory of Colonial Modes of Production." *Economic and Political Weekly* 7, no. 52 (December 23, 1972): 2498–2502.

————. "Modes of Production in a Materialist Conception of History." *Capital and Class* 3 (Autumn 1977): 1–44.

Baran, P. and Sweezy, P. M. *Monopoly Capital*. New York, 1966.

Bamat, T. "Relative State Autonomy and Capitalism in Brazil and Peru." *Insurgent Sociologist* 7, no. 2: 74–84.

Bettelheim, C. "State Property and Socialism." *Economy and Society* 2, no. 4 (1973).

Blackburn, R., ed. *Ideology In Social Science*. London, 1972.

Blanke, B., Jurgens, U., and Kastendiek, H. "On the Current Marxist Discussion on the Analysis of Form and Function of the Bourgeois State." In *State and Capital*, edited by J. Holloway and S. Picciotto. London, 1978.

Bobbio, N. "Are There Alternatives to Representative Democracy?" *Telos* 35 (Spring 1978): 17–30.

————. "Is There a Marxist Theory of the State?" *Telos* 35 (Spring 1978): 5–16.

Borón, A. "Latin America: Between Hobbes and Friedman." *New Left Review* 130 (November–December 1981): 45–66.

————. "New Forms of Capitalist State in Latin America: An Exploration." *Race and Class* 20, no. 3 (Winter 1979): 263–76.

Brus, W. "The Polish October—Twenty Years Later." *Socialist Register,* edited by R. Miliband and J. Saville. New York and London, 1977.

Cardoso, F. H. "Associated Dependent Development: Theoretical and Practical Implications." In A. Stephen, ed., *Authoritarian Brazil: Origins, Politics and Future.* New Haven, 1973.

———— and Faletto, E. "Estado y proceso politica én America Latina." *Rev. Max. de Sociologia* (April–June 1977).

Chaliand, G. *Revolution in the Third World: Myths and Prospects.* Brighton, 1977.

Chichilnisky, G. *et al.* "Authoritarianism and Development: A Global Perspective." *International Foundation for Development Alternatives* 19 (September/October 1980): 3–14.

Chinchilla, N. S. "Class Struggle in Central America: Background and Overview." *Latin America Perspectives* 7, nos. 2 and 3 (Spring and Summer 1980).

Collier, D., ed. *The New Authoritarianism in Latin America.* Princeton, 1979.

Cueva, A. "Fascismo y economía on America Latina." *Controversia* (Mexico) 1, no. 2 (1977): 37–43.

————. "The Latin American State in the Crisis of Capitalism." In *II Congress of Third World Economists.* Havana, 1981.

Debray, R. *Critique of Arms.* Harmondsworth, 1975.

————. *Revolution in the Revolution.* New York, 1968.

Draper, H. *Karl Marx's Theory of Revolution,* Part I. New York and London, 1977.

Engels, F. *Anti-Dühring.* Moscow, 1962.

Entralgo, A. "Notes on the Social Structure of Black Africa." *Tricontinental* (Havana) 68, 69, and 70 (1980).

Fine, B. and Harris, L. "State Expenditure in Advanced Capitalism: A Critique." *New Left Review* 98 (1976).

Fitzgerald, E. V. "State Capitalism in Peru." *Boletin de Estudios Latin Americanos y del Caribe* 20 (1976): 17–33.

————. *The State in Economic Development.* Cambridge, 1976.

Foster-Carter, A. "The Modes of Production Controversy." *New Left Review* 107 (1978): 47–77.

————. "Neo-Marxist Approaches to Development and Underdevelopment." In *Sociology of Development,* edited by E. de Kadt and G. Williams. London, 1974.

Frank, A. G. *Capitalism and Underdevelopment in Latin America.* New York, 1967.

————. "Dependence Is Dead, Long Live Dependency and the Class Struggle." *World Development* 5, no. 4 (1977): 355–70.

————. "Super Exploitation in the Third World." *Two-Thirds* 1, no. 2, pp. 15–28.

Gerstenberger, H. "Class Conflict, Competition and State Functions." In *State and Capital*, edited by J. Holloway and S. Picciotto. London, 1978.

Girling, S. "The State in Post-Colonial Societies—Pakistan and Bangladesh. Comments on Hamza Alavi." *Kapitalistate* 2 (1973): 49–51.

Gittens, T. W. "The Post-Colonial State, Class Formation, and Social Transformation: A Return to Theory." *Transition* (forthcoming).

Gold, D., et al. "Recent Developments in Marxist Theories of the Capitalist State." *Monthly Review* 27, no. 5 (1975): 29–43.

Gough, I. "State Expenditure in Advanced Capitalism." *New Left Review* 92 (1975): 53–92.

Goulbourne, H. *Politics and State in the Third World.* London, 1979.

Gramsci, A. *Selections from the Prison Notebooks.* London and New York, 1975.

Green, C. A. "Toward a Theory of Colonial Modes of Production: A Marxist Approach" M. A. thesis, University of Toronto, 1980.

Hamilton, N. "Dependent Capitalism and the State: The Case of Mexico." *Kapitalistate* 3 (1975): 72–82.

Hammergran, L. "Corporatism in Latin American Politics." *Comparative Politics* 9, no. 4 (July 1977): 443–61.

Harnecker, M. "Nicaragua: The Strategy of Victory (Interview with FSLN Commander H. Ortega)." *Intercontinental Press*, February 18, 1980.

Hein, W. and Stenzel, K. "The Capitalist State and Underdevelopment in Latin America." *Kapitalistate* 2 (1973): 31–48.

Held, D. and Kreiger, J. "Theories of the State." In *The State in Capitalist Europe*, edited by S. Bernstein et al. London, 1982.

Henderson, B. "The Chilean State After the Coup." In *Socialist Register 1977*, edited by R. Miliband and J. Saville. New York and London, 1977.

Hirsch, J. "The State Apparatus and Social Reproduction: Elements of a Theory of the Bourgeois State." In *State and Capital*, edited by J. Holloway and S. Picciotto. London, 1978.

Holloway, J. and Picciotto, S. "Introduction: Toward a Materialist Theory of the State." In *State and Capital*, edited by J. Holloway and S. Picciotto. London, 1978.

————. "A Note on the Theory of State (a reply to Ian Gough)." *Bulletin of the Conference of Socialist Economists* 14 (1976).

Hunt, A., ed. *Marxism and Democracy.* London, 1980.

Jessop, B. *The Capitalist State.* Oxford, 1982.

————. "Recent Theories of the Capitalist State." *Cambridge Journal of Economics* 1, no. 4 (1977).

Jung, H. "Behind the Nicaragua Revolution." New Left Review 117 (1979): 69–70.

Klare, M. T. Supplying Repression: U.S. Support for Authoritarian Regimes Abroad. Washington, D.C., 1977.

Laclau, E. "The Specificity of the Political: The Poulantzas-Miliband Debate." Economy and Society 4, no. 1 (1975): 87–110.

Leys, C. "The Overdeveloped Post-Colonial State: A Re-Evaluation." Review of Radical Political Economy (January–April 1976): 39–48.

Lieuwen, E. "Militarism and Politics in Latin America." In The Role of the Military in Underdeveloped Societies, edited by J. J. Johnson. Princeton, 1962.

Linz, J. I. "Totalitarian and Authoritarian Regimes." In Handbook of Political Science, edited by E. Greenstein and N. Polsby. Reading, Mass., 1975.

Lutchman, H. A. "From Colonialism to Cooperative Republic (Aspects of Political Development in Guyana)." Institute of Caribbean Studies, University of Puerto Rico, 1974.

Luxemburg, Rosa. The Russian Revolution. Ann Arbor, 1961.

Magdoff, H. Imperialism: From the Colonial Age to the Present. New York and London, 1978.

Malloy, J., ed. Authoritarianism and Corporatism in Latin America. Pittsburgh, 1977.

Mamdani, M. Politics and Class Formation in Uganda. New York and London, 1976.

Mandel, E. Marxist Economic Theory. London and New York, 1962.

––––––. "The Nature of the Soviet State." New Left Review 108 (1978): 23–46.

Meszaros, I. "Dictatorship and Dissent." New Left Review 108 (1978): 3–22.

Miliband, R. "The Capitalist State: A Reply to Nicos Poulantzas." New Left Review 59 (1970): 53–60.

––––––. "Poulantzas and the Capitalist State." New Left Review 82 (1973).

––––––. The State in Capitalist Society. London, 1969.

––––––. "State Power and Class Interests." New Left Review 138 (March–April 1983): 57–68.

Mires, F. "Para una critica de la teoria del fascismo Latinoamericana." Nueva Sociedad 45 (November/December 1979): 22–49.

Mollenkoph, J. "Theories of State and Power Structure Research." Insurgent Sociologist 3 (1975).

Moore, B., Jr. Social Origins of Dictatorship and Democracy. Boston, 1966.

Muller, W. and Neussus, C. "The Welfare-State Illusion and the Contradiction Between Wage Labour and Capital." In State and Capital, edited by J. Holloway and S. Picciotto. London, 1978.

Munck, R. "State Intervention in Brazil: Issues and Debates." Latin American Perspectives 7, no. 4 (Fall 1979): 16–31.

Munroe, T. and Robotham, D. *Struggles of the Jamaican People*. Kingston, 1977.

Myllnaki, E. "The Problems of Militarism in Latin America." *Ibero Americana* (Stockholm) 7, no. 2 and 8, no. 1 (1978): 68–76.

Needler, M. "The Logic of Conspiracy: The Latin American Military Coup as a Problem in the Social Sciences." *Studies in Comparative Development* 13, no. 3 (Fall 1978): 28–40.

O'Brien, P. "The Emperor Has No Clothes: Class and State in Latin America." Paper presented at the conference on "The State and Economic Development," Cambridge University, 1976.

O'Donnell, G. *Modernization and Bureaucratic Authoritarianism*. Berkeley, Ca., 1973.

Offe, C. "The Abolition of Market Control and the Problem of Legitimacy." *Kapitalistate* 1 (May 1973): 109–116 and 2 (December–January 1974): 73–75.

————. "Political Authority and Class Structures: An Analysis of Late Capitalist Societies." *International Journal of Sociology* 2, no. 1 (Spring 1972): 73–108.

————. "The Theory of the Capitalist State and the Problem of Policy Formation." In *Stress and Contradiction in Modern Capitalism*, edited by L. Lindberg et al. Lexington, Mass., 1975.

Othman, H. "The Tanzanian State." *Monthly Review* 26, no. 7 (December 1974): 46–57.

Panitch, L. "The Development of Corporatism in Liberal Democracies." *Comparative Political Studies* 10, no. 1 (1977).

Parge, J. *Agrarian Revolution*. New York, 1975.

Petras, J. *Critical Perspectives on Imperialism and Social Class in the Third World*. New York and London, 1978.

Pompermayer, M. J. "The State and Dependent Development." *Kapitalistate* 1 (1973): 25–27.

Poulantzas, N. "The Capitalist State: A Reply to Miliband and Laclau." *New Left Review* 95 (1976).

————. *The Crisis of Dictatorship*. London, 1976.

————. *Political Power and Social Classes*. London, 1973.

————. "The Problems of the Capitalist State." *New Left Review* 58 (1969): 67–78.

————. *State, Power, and Socialism*. London, 1980.

————. "Towards a Democratic Socialism." *New Left Review* 109 (1978): 75–87.

Reichelt, H. "Some Comments on Flatow and Huisken's Essay on the Problem of the Derivation of the Bourgeois State." In *State and Capital*, edited by J. Holloway and S. Picciotto. London, 1978.

Roxborough, I. *Theories of Underdevelopment*. London, 1979.

Saul, J. S. "The State in Post-Colonial Societies: Tanzania." *Socialist Register 1974*. London, 1974.

————. *State and Revolution in East Africa: Essays*. New York and London, 1979.

150   *The Rise of the Authoritarian State*

————. "The Unsteady State: Uganda, Obote, and General Amin." *Review of African Political Economy* (January–April 1976).
Sawer, M. "The Genesis of State and Revolution." In *Socialist Register 1977*, edited by R. Miliband and J. Saville. New York and London, 1977.
Shirokov, G. "Interstructural Relations in Developing Countries Economy." *Social Sciences* 4 (1980): 139–50.
Shivji, I. *Class Struggles in Tanzania*. New York and London, 1976.
Stanis, et al. *The Role of the State in the Socio-Economic Reform of the Developing Countries*. Moscow, 1976.
Stone, C. "Decolonization and the Caribbean State System: The Case of Jamaica." Center for Inter-American Relations, New York, 1978.
Sweezy, P. "Socialism in Poor Countries." *Monthly Review* 28, no. 5 (October 1976): 1–13.
Therborn, G. "The Rule of Capital and the Rise of Democracy." *New Left Review* 103 (May–June 1977).
————. "The Travail of Latin American Democracy." *New Left Review* 113–114 (January–April 1979).
Thomas, Clive Y. *Dependence and Transformation*. New York and London, 1974.
————. "From Colony to State Capitalism." *Transition*, forthcoming.
————. "The Non-Capitalist Path as Theory and Practice of Decolonization and Socialist Transformation." *Latin American Perspectives* 17 (Spring 1977): 10–28.
————. "On Formulating a Marxist Theory of Regional Integration." *Transition* 1, no. 1 (1978): 59–71.
————. *Plantations, Peasants, and the State: A Study of the Modes of Sugar Production in Guyana*. ILO–University of Guyana, forthcoming.
————. "Socialist-Capitalist Economic Relations and the Struggle for a New International Economic Order." *Transition* 2, no. 1 (1979): 1–20.
————. "State Capitalism in Guyana: An Assessment of Burnham's Cooperative Socialist Republic." In *Crisis in the Caribbean*, edited by F. Ambursley and R. Cohen. New York, 1984.
Thompson, E. "The Secret State." *Race and Class* 20, no. 3 (Winter 1979): 219–42.
Wallerstein, I. "The State and Social Transformation." *Politics and Society* 1 (1971): 359–64.
Warren, W. *Imperialism: Pioneer of Capitalism*. London, 1980.
Von Braunmuhl, C. "On the Analysis of the Bourgeois Nation State within the World Market Context." In *State and Capital*, edited by J. Holloway and S. Picciotto. London, 1978.
Woddis, J. *New Theories of Revolution*. New York, 1972.
Ziemann, W. and Lanzendörfer, M. "The State in Peripheral Societies." In *Socialist Register 1977*, edited by R. Miliband and J. Saville. New York and London, 1977.

Index

Accumulation: crisis of, 38–39, 93; forms of, 37, 86–87, 129; internal, 34, 42, 53–54; primitive, 30

Afghanistan, xxv

Africa, xvii, 14, 19, 58, 63, 95; class structure in, 64; colonial domination of, xix, xx, 21, 29; nationalist movement in, xxv, 38

Agriculture, xxiii, 11, 27, 29, 32, 56; diversification in, 30, 41; plantation economy, 12–13; state role in, 51

Ahmad, Egbal, 90

Alavi, Hamza, xvii, 71–73

Alliance of progressive forces, xxiii; need for, in defeat of authoritarian state, 130–31, 133, 134–36

Althusser, Louis, 118

Amerindians, 10, 22, 23

Amin, Idi, xiii, xx, 128

Anglicization, xxi-xxii

Anti-imperialism, 38, 39, 40, 54, 77, 84

Appropriation of surplus value, 8–9, 10, 11–12, 13–14; direct, by state, 85–86; from periphery to center, 30, 94

Argentina, 109

Asia, xvii, xix, 63, 87, 89; nationalist movement in, 38; political domination of, 29

Australia, xx, 19, 38

Authoritarian state, xiv, xx–xxi, 45, 67, 119, 129, 135–36; alliances of forces needed to defeat, 129–36; bureaucratic authoritarianism and, 109–12; diagnosis of, 133–34; distinct from fascism, 105–9; ideology and, 119–27; inherent instability

of, 96–97; international context of, 93–94; material basis of, 83–88, 89, 92; methods of rule, 83, 88–92, 95, 100; as product of conjuncture of world and peripheral capitalist development, 88, 93, 111, 125; rise of, 82–112; significant features of, 128–29; unpopularity of, 97, 123–24

Banaji, J., 14

Bangladesh, 71

Bobbio, N., xvi, xviii, 103–4

Bokassa, Jean Bedel, xx

Bourgeois-democratic state, xvi–xvii, xxi, 90, 94, 119; ideology in, 117

Bourgeoisie, xxvi, 84, 106, 112; Great Britain, 28, 31; industrial, 58; Latin America, 110–11. See also Petty bourgeoisie

Brazil, 19, 53, 109, 111, 128

Bureaucracy, 53, 74, 88, 90–91

Bureaucratic authoritarianism; and authoritarian state, 109–12

Burma, xxv

Burnham, Forbes, xxii

Canada, xx, 38

Capital, 31, 85–86; export of, 28, 37; foreign, 42, 52, 54, 62, 77, 107; local, 62, 66, 77

Capitalism, 37, 39, 69; center-periphery, 27–36, 62; colonial mediation of, 11–14, 29; ideology of, 42, 125–27; industrial, 11, 13–14; Marxian analysis of, 71–72, 73; political democracy under, 99–102

Capitalism as world system, 66, 88; place of periphery in, xx, 84, 93;

Postcolonial (concept), xviii, xix

Postcolonial state, xiv, xv, xvii, xviii, 43, 45, 49, 112; methods of rule, 50–54; political legitimacy of, 54–56

Poulantzas, Nicos, xvi, 104, 117–18

Power: concentration of, 14–15; geographical distribution of, 54; political flowed from economic, 24, 62; public, 15, 16

Production: export-oriented primary, 2, 3, 42, 86, 87; private sector, 70, 114, 117, 119

Profits, 28, 31, 38; speculative, 12

Proletariat: Latin America, 111; underdeveloped, 84. See also Dictatorship of the proletariat

Propertied classes, 71, 97; Latin America, 110–11; postcolonial state, 58–64

Public opinion: manipulation of, 123, 124

Racism, 23, 25

Repression, xiii, xiv, xv, xxii, xxv, 97, 103, 123–24, 128–29; authoritarian state, 89–92; capitalist state, 117–18; ideology and, 120; by military, 110

Resource use, 41–42

Rights, 20, 99, 100. See also Freedoms; Human rights

Rule of law, 35, 82

Ruling class, 55, 88, 93, 136; authoritarian state as response of, 128, 129; capitalist countries, 100; colonial state, 20–21, 22, 24, 25, 30, 31, 68 (see also Planter class); direct rule by, 20–21, 24; fascist state, 106–7, 108–9; foreigners in, 64; fractionalized, 69–70, 71–72, 73–74, 76, 80; lack of clearly hegemonic, in periphery, 65–66, 71; petty bourgeoisie as, 60–61; relation of, to state, 7–8, 74, 76, 79; resistance to autonomy of state, 79–80; use of ideology to maintain hegemony, 82–83, 113, 114, 115, 116, 117, 118–19, 122–23, 125

Saul, John, xvii, 73, 119

Security services, 91; political personnel in, 89–90

Shivji, Issa, xvii; Class Struggles in Tanzania, 61

Slave trade, 9; abolition of, 18, 19

Slavery, 1, 3–17, 18; abolition of, 3, 18, 19–20, 24, 25; and state, 14–17

Social consciousness: forms of, 115–16

Social-democratic path, xxiii, xxv, 80, 135–36

Social relations, 4, 63, 72, 86; democratization of, xxiii, xxv; periphery, 30, 37, 64; state regulation of, 5–6; transformation of internal, 31–33

Social reproduction, 83–88; state role in, 73, 76

Social structure, 18–19, 34, 65, 84; and class, 49, 56–64; in fascism, 108

Socialism, xvi, xxiii, 96, 132; global conflict with capitalism, 39; in periphery, xvi, 54, 80, 98–104; political democracy and, 83, 98–109; pseudo, in ideology, 121–22; in Soviet Union, 39; transformation into, 130, 135–36; transition to, xv, xxiv

Socialist bloc, 132, 134

South Africa, 38

South Korea, 28

South Yemen, xxv

Sovereignty, 5, 111, 112

Soviet bloc, xxii

Soviet Union, 39, 50

Spain, 11, 19, 39

Standard of Living, xiv, 39, 88, 105

State, xiv, xv, xxv, 4, 13, 15–16, 79, 89, 119; centrality of, 73, 119; class basis of, 7–8, 79, 97, 101; class structure and, in periphery, 49–66; complementarity of ideological relations with, 114–15; consolidation of, 30–31; as employer, 57–58, 62, 66, 85–86; equated with society, 120; expansion of, 51, 54–55; functions of, 5–6, 11, 33–34, 50–54, 76–77, 108, 110; ideological and cultural apparatuses of, 35–36, 73, 82–83; impact of colonialism and slavery on, 1, 3–17; as internally and externally determined, 16–17; interventionist, 7, 22, 52–54, 58, 129; mediating among ruling-class